Celebrity

Focus on Contemporary Issues (FOCI) addresses the pressing problems, ideas and debates of the new millennium. Subjects are drawn from the arts, sciences and humanities, and are linked by the impact they have had or are having on contemporary culture. FOCI books are intended for an intelligent, alert audience with a general understanding of, and curiosity about, the intellectual debates shaping culture today. Instead of easing readers into a comfortable awareness of particular fields, these books are combative. They offer points of view, take sides and are written with passion.

SERIES EDITORS
Barrie Bullen and Peter Hamilton

In the same series

Brit-myth
Chris Rojek

Anarchism
Seán M. Sheehan

Cool Rules
Dick Pountain and David Robins

The Happiness Paradox
Ziyad Marar

Chromophobia
David Batchelor

First Peoples
Jeffrey Sissons

Global Dimensions
John Rennie Short

Contemporary Gothic
Catherine Spooner

Activism!
Tim Jordan

Stalking
Bran Nicol

Animal
Erica Fudge

Retro
Elizabeth E. Guffey

Dreamtelling
Pierre Sorlin

Celebrity

CHRIS ROJEK

REAKTION BOOKS

For Ian and Alison Eastment,
celebrities in their own fashion

Published by Reaktion Books Ltd
33 Great Sutton Street
London EC1V ODX, UK

www.reaktionbooks.co.uk

First published 2001
Transferred to digital printing 2010

Designed by Libanus Press
Printed and bound by University of Chicago Press

British Library Cataloguing in Publishing Data
Rojek, Chris
    Celebrity. – (FOCI)
    1. Fame 2. Celebrities
    I. Title
    306.4

ISBN 978 186189 104 4

Contents

1 Celebrity and Celetoids   9

2 Celebrity and Religion   51

3 Celebrity and Aestheticization   101

4 Celebrity and Transgression   143

5 Celebrity and Celebrification   181

References   200

Bibliography   204

Acknowledgements   206

List of Illustrations   208

The intellect cannot conquer vanity. Nor is it an accident that the word 'vanity' is close to 'void'.
Leszek Kolakowski, philosopher and social theorist

This new look is a cross between polka dots and skin rash ... simulating infection and disease. I've done it this way because I still like wearing make-up but I don't want to be a gender bender ... basically I never want to look ordinary.
Leigh Bowery, Anglo-Australian performance artist, and celebrated model for the painter Lucien Freud

To do is to be (Marx)
To be is to do (Sartre)
Do be do be do (Sinatra)
Student graffiti

CHAPTER ONE

Celebrity and Celetoids

Although God-like qualities are often attributed to celebrities, the modern meaning of the term *celebrity* actually derives from the fall of the gods, and the rise of democratic governments and secular societies. This is no accident. The increasing importance of the public face in everyday life is a consequence of the rise of public society, a society that cultivates personal style as the antidote to formal democratic equality. The Latin root of the term is *celebrem*, which has connotations with both 'fame' and 'being thronged'. There is also a connection in Latin with the term *celere*, from which the English word *celerity* derives, meaning 'swift'. The Latin roots indicate a relationship in which a person is marked out as possessing singularity, and a social structure in which the character of fame is fleeting. The French word *célèbre*, meaning 'well known in public', carries similar connotations. In addition, it suggests representations of fame that flourish beyond the boundaries of religion and Court society. In a word, it ties celebrity to a *public*, and acknowledges the fickle, temporary nature of the market in human sentiments. These are prominent themes in contemporary social theory. Indeed, modernity is often understood as a condition

9

defined by the spread of episodic, anonymous relations in culture, and the increasing speed of change in social and economic life.

In this book I treat celebrity as the attribution of glamorous or notorious status to an individual within the public sphere. Several caveats must be added to this definition. First, glamour and notoriety are usually thought of in polarized terms. The Brazilian model Gisele Bundchen is glamorous; Timothy McVeigh, the Oklahoma City bomber, is notorious. Glamour is associated with favourable public recognition. Notoriety is unfavourable public recognition. Notoriety is a sub-branch of celebrity culture, and, arguably, an increasingly important one. Leaving moral considerations aside, what connects Bundchen to McVeigh is cultural impact. We might reduce this to an admittedly rather crude equation: celebrity = impact on public consciousness. The equation will certainly have to be modified in what follows, but as a starting point it will help to focus the discussion on what, today, is justly described as the public addiction to celebrity. Why do so many of us measure our worth against figures we have never met? Why is the desire for fame so widespread among ordinary people? The answers have something to do with the way that public life is constructed. The media determine this idiom, although the content remains a matter of political and ideological exchange. The scheduling of emotions, presentation of self in interpersonal relations and techniques of public impression management, which employ media celebrities to humanize and dramatize them, permeate ordinary social relationships.

Second, the question of who is attributing celebrity status is moot. Celebrities are cultural fabrications. Their impact on the public may appear to be intimate and spontaneous. In fact, celebrities are carefully mediated through what might be termed chains of attraction. No celebrity now acquires public recognition without the assistance of cultural intermediaries who operate to stage-manage celebrity presence in the eyes of the public. 'Cultural intermediaries' is the collective term for agents, publicists, marketing personnel, promoters, photographers, fitness trainers, wardrobe staff, cosmetics experts and personal assistants. Their task is to concoct the public presentation of celebrity personalities that will result in an enduring appeal for the audience of fans. This holds good for the public presentation of notorious celebrities. The fiction of James Ellroy and Jake Arnott spins a mantle of glamour around notorious historical celebrity figures like Lee Harvey Oswald, Sam Giancano and Reggie and Ronnie Kray. In the 1990s, movie directors like Quentin Tarantino and Guy Ritchie, now Madonna'a husband, glamorized the Underworld in films like *Reservoir Dogs, Pulp Fiction, Jackie Brown, Lock, Stock & Two Smoking Barrels* and *Snatch.*

Third, celebrity status always implies a split between a private self and a public self. The social psychologist George Herbert Mead argued that the split between the *I* (the 'veridical' self) and the *Me* (the self as seen by others) is the human condition, at least since ancient times, in Western society.[1] The public presentation of self is always a staged activity, in which the human actor presents a 'front' or 'face' to others while keeping a significant portion of the self in reserve. For the celebrity, the split between the I and the Me is often disturbing. So much so, that celebrities frequently complain of identity confusion and the colonization of the veridical self by the public face. Cary Grant dealt with this ironically by remarking that he, like his audience, would love to be like Cary Grant, by which he meant that even he acknowledged the split between his public face and his veridical self. Other celebrities suffer a clinical or sub-clinical loss of identity. For example, Peter Sellers complained that he 'disappeared' once a film role ended. This suggests that his sense of veridical self was virtually extinguished. Contrarily, the veridical self may make increasingly desperate attempts to overcome the tyranny of the public face. This may result in a pathological slippage between the I and the Me, as the public face resorts to more dramatic attempts in order to alert the public to the horror, shame and encroaching helplessness of the veridical self. Keith Moon, The Who's former drummer, and the late film star Oliver Reed are examples of chronic identity slippage. This may be understood as a pathological condition, since the public face of both celebrities became increasingly dependent on alcohol and, in Moon's case, drugs too.

Of course, the desire to transcend the veridical self is often the chief motive behind the struggle to achieve celebrity status. Johnny Depp, during the filming of *Sleepy Hollow* (1999), is reported to have attacked photographers at a London restaurant for their intrusion, complaining that 'I don't want to be what you want me to be tonight.' A notable paradox of fame is that this desire frequently culminates in either a sense of engulf-ment by a public face that is regarded as alien to the veridical self or, worse, a sense of personal extinction in the 'face' of others who treat the veridical self as 'inauthentic'.

Fourth, a distinction should be made between celebrity, notoriety and renown. *Renown*, in this book, refers to the informal attribution of distinc-tion on an individual within a given social network. Thus, in every social group certain individuals stand out by virtue of their wit, beauty, courage, prowess, achievements or grace. Renown, you might say, depends on recip-rocal personal or direct para-social contact. These individuals have a sort of localized fame within the particular social assemblage of which they are a part. In contrast, the fame of the celebrity is ubiquitous. One peculiar tension in celebrity culture is that the arousal of strong emotion is attained despite the absence of direct, personal reciprocity. Whereas renown follows from personal contact with the individual who is differentiated as unusual or unique, celebrity and notoriety assume a relationship in which the individual who is differentiated by honorific status is distanced from the spectator by stage, screen or some equivalent medium of communica-tion. Social distance is the precondition of both celebrity and notoriety. This frequently leads to friction in the management of inter-personal rela-tions between celebrities, spouses, children and kin. Those who command public acclaim and desire often suffer severe distress when approval is not demonstrated in private life. Elizabeth Taylor, Frank Sinatra, Jayne

Mansfield, Ernest Hemingway, Richard Burton and Judy Garland all married and divorced several times, and appear to have experienced difficulties when seeking to establish a stable relationship.

Celebrity, the Media and Celebrification

I focus on attribution and distance rather than the innate qualities or characteristics of celebrity because I believe that mass-media representation is the key principle in the formation of celebrity culture. To us, celebrities often seem magical or superhuman. However, that is because their presence in the public eye is comprehensively staged. One of the best examples of this is also one of the first publicity stunts of the film age. In March 1910, the Biograph Film Company announced the tragic and untimely death of one of its brightest stars, Florence Lawrence. In fact, Lawrence was alive and well, and her subsequent appearance in St Louis won the film company unprecedented publicity.

The emergence of celebrity as a public preoccupation is the result of three major interrelated historical processes. First, the democratization of society; second, the decline in organized religion; third, the commodification of everyday life. Each of these three themes will be elaborated in what follows. It is sufficient to say at this point that the decline of Court society in the seventeenth and eighteenth centuries involved the transference of cultural capital to self-made men and women. As modern society developed, celebrities have filled the absence created by the decay in the popular belief in the divine right of kings, and the death of God. The American Revolution sought to overthrow not merely the institutions of colonialism but the ideology of monarchical power too. It replaced them with an alternative ideology, in some ways no less flawed and fantastic: the ideology of the common man. This ideology legitimated the political system and sustained business and industry, thus contributing immensely to the commodification of celebrity. Celebrities replaced the monarchy as the new symbols of recognition and belonging, and as the belief in God waned, celebrities became immortal. This is why, for example, Thomas Jefferson, George Washington, Gandhi and Winston Churchill retain an immense aura in contemporary culture. It is also why John Wayne, dead for over 20 years, is still regularly voted to be one of the most popular movie stars in America; and why Rudolph Valentino, Elvis Presley, Marilyn Monroe, John F. Kennedy, James Dean, John Lennon, Jim Morrison, Tupac Shakur and Kurt Cobain remain idols of cult worship. Politically and culturally, the ideology of the common man elevated the public sphere as the arena *par excellence*, in which the dramatic personality and achieved style inscribed distinction and grabbed popular attention. To this extent, celebrity culture provides an important integrating function in secular society.

At the same time, the desire mobilized by celebrity culture is abstract. The logic of capitalist accumulation requires consumers to constantly exchange their wants. The restlessness and friction in industrial culture partly derives from the capitalist requirement to initiate perpetual commodity and brand innovation. In such circumstances desire is *alienable*, transferable, since wants must be perpetually switched in response to market developments. The market inevitably turned the public face of the celebrity into a commodity. We will not understand the peculiar hold that celebrities exert over us today unless we recognize that celebrity culture is irrevocably bound up with commodity culture. In chapter Five I will take up the implications of this.

But consumers are not merely part of a market of commodities, they are also part of a market of sentiments. Capitalist organization requires individuals to be both desiring objects and objects of desire. For economic growth depends on the consumption of commodities, and cultural integration depends on the renewal of the bonds of social attraction. Celebrities humanize the process of commodity consumption. Celebrity culture has emerged as a central mechanism in structuring the market of human sentiments. Celebrities are commodities in the sense that consumers desire to possess them. Interestingly, this point extends to notorious celebrity figures. The serial killers Ian Brady, Myra Hindley, Rosemary West, Jeffrey Dahmer, Ted Bundy, Harold Shipman and Timothy McVeigh were all deluged with fan mail while in prison. McVeigh, who was executed on 11 June 2001, had received four proposals of marriage. Far from being reviled and outcast, notorious celebrities are cherished as necessary folk devils by significant layers of the public.

It is easy to see why mainstream celebrities feed the everyday world with honorific standards of attraction that encourage people to emulate them, which helps to cement and unify society. *Prima facie*, it is less easy to understand the fan base for notorious celebrities. Except, perhaps, when one places the notorious celebrity in the context of democracy, with its equalizing functions, its timorous disdain for extremity and its grey affirmation of equal rights and responsibilities. In such a context, the figure of notoriety possesses colour, instant cachet, and may even, in some circles, be invested with heroism for daring to release the emotions of blocked aggression and sexuality that civilized society seeks to repress.

If celebrity society possesses strong tendencies to make us covet celebrities, and to construct ourselves into objects that immediately arouse sentiments of desire and approval in others, it also creates many more losers than winners. The celebrity race is now so ubiquitous in all walks of life that living with failure is oppressive for those of us who do not become achieved celebrities. In extreme cases, people who do not attain achieved celebrity resort to violent behaviour in order to acquire acclaim. Chapter Four examines the relationship between notoriety and celebrity. It examines the role of the celebrity race in the growth of stalkers and makes connections between the search for celebrity and some forms of murder and serial killing.

In the final chapter I introduce the concept of the 'celebrification process' to encapsulate the ubiquitous character of celebrity in everyday life. I argue that, with the growth of unified markets and a pervasive system of mass communication, culture has gradually become mediagenic. The evening news on TV brings together more people than all editions of the national newspapers combined. Everyday social and cultural exchange utilizes the styles, points of view, conversational prompts and steering agendas supplied by the media. Of course, these are inflected, revised and recast by the direct circumstances and relations of life in which we are located. None the less, it is reasonable to propose that media influence is a major factor in everyday inter-personal exchange; further, that celebrities are significant nodal points of articulation between the social and the personal. Hence, celebrity must be understood as a *modern* phenomenon, a phenomenon of mass-circulation newspapers, TV, radio and film.

The sociologist Pierre Bourdieu is caustic about the power of media celebrities. 'Our news anchors', he complains, 'our talk show hosts, and our sports announcers ... are always telling us what we "should think" about what they call "social problems", such as violence in the inner city or in the schools.'[2] One might object that this view is too one-dimensional. The influence of media celebrities is more nuanced, notably in respect of replenishing democracy through informing the public and renewing public accountability, than Bourdieu allows. Even so, his point – which is that popular and, to a large degree, personal culture is now mediagenic, both in respect of the presentation of personality in everyday exchange and the setting of life goals – is valid. Celebrification proposes that ordinary identity formation and general forms of social interaction are patterned and inflected by the styles, embodied attitudes and conversational flow developed through celebrity culture. Celebrities simultaneously embody social types and provide role models.

The fact that media representation is the basis of celebrity is at the heart of both the question of the mysterious tenacity of celebrity power and the peculiar fragility of celebrity presence. From the perspective of the audience, it makes celebrities seem, simultaneously, both larger than life and intimate confrères. Staging presence through the media inevitably raises the question of authenticity. This is a perpetual dilemma for both the celebrity and the audience. Out-of-face encounters between celebrities and fans tend to produce three results. (By the term *out of face* I mean interaction between a celebrity and an audience in which the veridical self of the celebrity, or its lack, becomes ascendant, thus contradicting or disconfirming the pattern of expectations and reactions constructed around the public face.) The three results produced by this state of affairs are, first, *confirmation*, in which the public face of the celebrity is eventually regained and verified through direct interaction with fans. Second, *normalization*, in which celebrity status is rendered transparent through the articulation and recognition of common traits between the psychology and culture of celebrities and fans. By exposing the out-of-face side to personality, the celebrity momentarily becomes more like us. Recognition that celebrities are human after all often enhances public esteem. Elton John, Robert Downey Jnr, Boy George and Judy Garland each seem to have developed closer relations with the public after confessing to their battles with addiction. The third result is termed *cognitive dissonance*, wherein encounters radically conflict with mass-media images of celebrity, exposing the public face to critical condemnation as a calculated facade or prop.

Ascribed, Achieved and Attributed Celebrity

Celebrity status comes in three forms: *ascribed, achieved* and *attributed*. Ascribed celebrity concerns lineage: status typically follows from bloodline. The celebrity of Caroline Kennedy or Prince William stems from their line of biological descent. It is why kings and queens in earlier social formations commanded automatic respect and veneration. Individuals may add to or subtract from their ascribed status by virtue of their voluntary actions, but the foundation of their ascribed celebrity is predetermined.

In contrast, *achieved* celebrity derives from the perceived accomplishments of the individual in open competition. For example, Brad Pitt, Damien Hirst, Michael Jordan, Darcy Bussell, David Beckham, Lennox Lewis, Pete Sampras, Venus and Serena Williams and Monica Seles are celebrities by reason of their artistic or sporting achievements. In the public realm they are recognized as individuals who possess rare talents or skills.

However, achieved celebrity is not exclusively a matter of special talent or skill. In some cases it is largely the result of the concentrated representation of an individual as noteworthy or exceptional by cultural intermediaries. When this is so, it is *attributed* celebrity.

Why does celebrity follow from mere attribution? The main reason is the expansion of the mass-media. Sensationalism is the mass-media's response to the routines and predictabilities of everyday life. Daniel Boorstin coined the term 'pseudo-event' to refer to the arrangement of newsworthy events and personalities by publicists and newspaper editors.[3] Sensationalism aims to generate public interest with the object of galvanizing public attention. Thus, 'ordinary' people, like the British TV gardener Charlie Dimmock, Luciana Morad, the mother of one of Mick Jagger's illegitimate children, and Mandy Allwood, the British mother who was pregnant with octuplets, are vaulted into public consciousness as noteworthy figures, primarily at the behest of mass-media executives pursuing circulation or ratings wars. Later I shall introduce the term *celetoid* to refer to a media-generated, compressed, concentrated form of attributed celebrity.

It is frequently argued that media saturation means we now live in the age of the pseudo-event, with the result that the line between fact and fiction, reality and illusion has been erased. Perhaps this argument is hyperbolic, since its credibility rests ultimately on the exposure of many media topics as nothing more than orchestrated pseudo-events and the celetoid as an effect of media strategy. Once we recognize attributed celebrity as a category, we disarm the argument that the line between reality and illusion has been erased. Even so, the omnipresence of the mass-media require us to take the celetoid as an important category in contemporary culture.

One should add a caveat here. Of course, achieved celebrity pre-dated the rise of the mass-media. Bigots, forgers, criminals, whores, balladeers and thinkers have been objects of public attention since Greek and Roman times. They possessed what one might call *pre-figurative* celebrity status. That is, they were items of public discourse, and honorific or notorious status was certainly attributed to them. But they did not carry the illusion of intimacy, the sense of being an exalted confrère, that is part of celebrity status in the age of mass-media.

When strangers met John Wilmot, 2nd Earl of Rochester (1647–80), for the first time, they were generally unaware that they were in the company of a rake, a compulsive womanizer and the author of obscene satires against Charles II and his courtiers. These elements of the veridical self were secreted from the public view. As with nearly every pre-figurative celebrity, the fame of Rochester, who died young at 33 from syphilis, was posthumous. Arguably, historical figures like Rochester, Pocahontas, Titus Oates, Guy Fawkes, John Dee, Nell Gwyn and Gerard Winstanley enjoyed a measure of metropolitan celebrity in their lifetimes. But it was unevenly distributed. Its indispensable conduits were kinship and friendship circles and the possession of literacy. In contrast, the celebrity of the present age is ubiquitous, and possesses *élan vital* for a ravenous public audience. Unlike pre-figurative celebrity, the celebrity in contemporary society is accessible through internet sites, biographies, newspaper interviews, TV profiles, radio documentaries and film biographies. The veridical self is a site of perpetual public excavation.

Of course, celebrities often find this intrusive and, occasionally, insufferable. The desire that they mobilize in others is alienable. Strictly speaking, the public faces that celebrities construct do not belong to them, since they only possess validity if the public confirms them. The relationship of esteem is also one of dependency. Perhaps this accounts for the higher than average levels of neurosis and mental illness found among the celebritariat. Celebrities are literally elevated in public esteem, which frequently contributes to personal problems as they struggle to be 'themselves' with their families. A celebrity whose public face is rejected may fall prey to feelings of anxiety and mortification.

The fact that celebrity status depends on public recognition is ironic. A regular complaint made by celebrities is that the public has no respect for privacy. At the height of her fame, Greta Garbo retired from film and justified her decision by repeating for decades the mantra 'I want to be alone.' John Lennon explained Beatlemania in Britain as a reason for moving to Manhattan in 1970. In New York he felt he could walk the streets without being mobbed, although not, as it happened, without being shot dead. The deaths of Garbo and Lennon licensed deeper excavations of the veridical self by the media, much of it questionable, and some of it unsavoury. However, like every celebrity in contemporary society, their private lives were already part of the public domain, part of the insistent cultural data that we use to comprehend ourselves and to navigate through the crashing waves of the cultural sphere. Those who are successful in following the path of achieved or attributed celebrity surrender a portion of the veridical self, and leave the world of anonymity and privacy behind.

Celetoids and Celeactors

I propose *celetoid* as the term for any form of compressed, concentrated, attributed celebrity. I distinguish celetoids from celebrities because, generally, the latter enjoy a more durable career with the public. However, I take it for granted that many of the representational techniques that present celetoids and celebrities for public consumption are identical. Celetoids are the accessories of cultures organized around mass communications and staged authenticity. Examples include lottery winners, one-hit wonders, stalkers, whistle-blowers, sports' arena streakers, have-a-go-heroes, mistresses of public figures and the various other social types who command media attention one day, and are forgotten the next.

Consider James Bradley, Rene Gagnon and Ira Hayes. Who remembers them today? They were the three survivors of the team of six who raised the American flag in 1945 at Iwo Jima, during the 36-day battle in which 22,000 Japanese and 7,000 American soldiers perished. Joe Rosenthal's famous photograph seduced the imagination of the nation. When Bradley, Gagnon and Hayes returned home they were treated like royalty. The photograph was the inspiration for the famous patriotic bronze statue commemorating the war that was afterwards erected in Arlington Cemetery, Virginia, just across the Potomac river from Washington, DC. Bradley, who died in 1994, never discussed Iwo Jima. When Gagnon died at 54 he was working as a janitor, and bitter that his former celebrity had not translated into wealth. Perhaps most tragically of all, Hayes, who lived on an Indian reservation in Arizona, died from alcohol-related disease ten years after the famous photograph was taken.

It is in the nature of celetoids to receive their moment of fame and then to disappear from public consciousness quite rapidly. British readers may recall Ruth Lawrence, the adolescent prodigy who was a permanent fixture of the UK mass-media in the mid-1980s. In 1980 Ruth, at the age of 8, was the youngest person to have passed an O level. Aged 10, she was the youngest person to pass Oxford University's entrance exam. At 11 she began her degree, graduating at 13 with first-class honours. At 17 she gained her PhD. Ruth then emigrated to the USA, and the British press lost interest in her. For much of the 1990s she was at the University of Michigan, where she has gradually faded from celebrity status, opting instead for a low-profile role as mother and teacher.

The public elevation of, and concentration on, celetoids often follows public scandal. For example, Jessica Hahn became a celetoid after her affair with the televangelist Jim Bakker was exposed in 1987. She went on to pose twice for *Playboy* and launched her own 900 (sex) phone line. Gillian Flowers and Paula Jones became briefly famous after they alleged sexual relations with Bill Clinton. Monica Lewinsky became a global celetoid even before Clinton actually confessed his sexual relationship with her. Lewinsky received lucrative high-profile interviews on American TV and went on a world tour to promote her book. Darva Conger, a former emergency room nurse and Gulf War veteran, shot to fame in 2000 when she married a millionaire on the TV game-show *Who Wants to Marry a Millionaire?* The marriage soon ended in separation and Conger went on to pose for *Playboy*.

Celetoids are often constructed around sexual scandal, where they symbolize the hypocrisy or corruption of public figures. For example, the Profumo affair in Britain in the early 1960s, which twinned sexual intrigue involving a Cabinet minister with allegations of espionage, elevated the callgirls Christine Keeler and Mandy Rice Davies as fleeting celetoids, signalling the double standards of both prominent politicians and swinging London. More recently, the *doyen* of British publicists, Max Clifford, represented Antonia de Sancha, who claimed that the married Tory Cabinet Minister David Mellor made love to her wearing his beloved Chelsea FC strip. Clifford also represented the escort girl Pamela Bordes, who was alleged to have had affairs with Tory ministers as well as the newspaper editor Andrew Neil. In addition, Clifford organized luxury accommodation and the attentions of the *News of the World* for Mandy Allwood during her pregnancy with octuplets.

Evanescence is the irrevocable condition of celetoid status, though in exceptional cases a celetoid may acquire a degree of longevity. For example, Californians are used to the phenomenon of Angelyne, a pneumatic blonde, usually dressed in plunging leopard-skin, high heels and dark glasses, whose image was reproduced in gigantic billboards throughout Los Angeles in the 1980s and '90s. At first sight, Angelyne's image blatantly panders to sexist stereotypes. On the other hand, her poses are also ironical and reflexive. She resists monolithic readings based on sexual inequality. She is not famous for being a sex goddess, rather she is, as the cliché has it, famous for being famous. Her publicity stunts have led to TV interviews, a fan club numbering thousands and a walk-on appearance in the movie *Earth Girls Are Easy*. Her fame might best be comprehended as an artefact of kitsch culture.

By kitsch culture I mean a culture in which the conventions of normative order are established by the operations of manufactured novelties and planned sensations orchestrated by the mass-media. In setting the constructed nature of cultural identity and interaction as an *a priori* of normative public encounters, kitsch culture tacitly denies reality. Thus, Angelyne presents herself as arbitrarily famous, and therefore parodies the general constructed character of all forms of public celebrity.

An important sub-category of the celetoid is what I will call the *celeactor*. The celeactor is a fictional character who is either momentarily ubiquitous or becomes an institutionalized feature of popular culture. Like celetoids, celeactors are adjuncts of the mass-media. They cater to the public appetite for a character type that sums up the times.

In Britain, during the 1980s, Harry Enfield's celeactor, 'Loadsamoney', was the gross embodiment of Essex Man, the vulgar, *nouveau riche* materialist from cockney Essex whose values were popularized by Margaret Thatcher's government. At the start of 2000, the celeactor 'Ali G' began to occupy a similar place in the mass-media. Outwardly, Ali G (created and played by the Anglo-Jewish comic Sacha Baron Cohen) is a black British 'yoof' from Staines near London, who has declarative, but equivocal, connections with 'gangsta' culture. Part of the joke is that Ali G presents himself as a hip black Briton, although, in reality, Cohen obviously is not black, and Ali G has a questionable familiarity with black British–Jamaican values and *patois*. The name 'Ali' suggests that the character may in fact be of Asian descent, thus embedding another layer within the comedy of role and status confusion. Cohen plays Ali G cleverly, sometimes dangerously, pricking at both racial stereotyping and the sanctimony of political correctness. The comedy lies not only in Ali G's strident sincerity but also in the jaw-dropping credulity of the powerful, often rich, people he interviews, who take the Ali G character at face value. Thus, a prominent, and notably right-wing, former Conservative minister and headmaster is quizzed on the virtue of the metric system in the school curriculum, apparently without realizing that Ali G's enthusiasm for metric measurement is driven entirely by his interest in recreational drug use. Similarly, a feminist academic is presented with outrageous, misogynist values, but cannot dismiss them as peremptorily as she might in a staffroom meeting because the personality uttering them is apparently only semi-educated, and is a representative of an ethnic minority to boot. Some sections of the media have criticized Cohen for perpetuating racist and sexist stereotypes. Yet a careful reading of Ali G reveals that the comedy operates to deflate cant and humbug, whether articulated by racists and sexists or by those elected to serve as our moral guardians.

Celeactors are invariably satirical creations. Their purpose is to deflate the sanctimony of public figures or to highlight allegations of moral bankruptcy in public life. As such, they are the direct descendants of the figures depicted in the sketches, prints and paintings of eighteenth- and nineteenth-century caricaturists such as William Hogarth, Thomas Rowlandson and Honoré Daumier, all of whom spiked the pomposities of their day.

The cartoon form is an extremely effective medium for the presentation of satires of contemporary life. For example, the *Blondie* cartoon comic strip is published in 55 countries and 35 languages. It was introduced in 1930 by the cartoonist Chic Young at the outset of the Great Depression. It deals with the travails of the Bumstead family – Blondie and Dagwood Bumstead and their children, Baby Dumpling (Alexander) and Cookie. The success of this strip is usually attributed to its focus on universal themes: love, marriage, parenthood, work, relaxation, eating and sleeping.

Similarly, the successful British cartoon *Andy Capp*, which portrays working-class life in North-East England, is also widely syndicated throughout the world, and deals with similar themes, albeit from a working-class perspective. These characters certainly achieved cultural impact, and to this extent they can be considered as variants of the celeactor category.

Walt Disney's animated cartoon creations are also widely credited with achieving considerable cultural impact. Mickey Mouse exemplifies generosity of spirit and acceptable wholesome subversiveness. Donald Duck embodies the determination to do good, and his temper-tantrums reveal the enormity of this ambition. Pluto encapsulates stoicism and guilelessness. *Superman* and *Batman* also present idealized representations of American heroism and the defence of justice. In the 1980s and '90s, animated cartoons like *Beavis and Butthead*, *The Simpsons* and *South Park* satirized the orthodox values and institutions of the moral majority in America and utilized new stereotypes of disaffected youth, the strains of multi-culturalism and the casualties of the American Dream.

The development of cyber-culture has demonstrated the versatility of the cartoon form and extended the range of celeactor figures in popular culture. Lara Croft, the all-action cyber-heroine created by the British computer company Eidos, has achieved global popularity. Lara is perhaps the first clearly distinguished cyber-icon of the computer games world. The inspiration for the '90s game icon was drawn in important ways from Stephen Spielberg's 1980s *Indiana Jones* movie series starring Harrison Ford. Lara Croft is therefore a case of a cyber-icon born from the success of a celeactor, which appears to confirm Baudrillard's well known and influential argument that simulation has replaced reality.[4] By way of giving a twist to this story, the film star Angelina Jolie plays the part of Lara in a film version of *Tomb Raider*.

Celebrity construction and presentation involve an imaginary public face. In the case of celeactors, there is no veridical self, and the public face is entirely a fictional creation. The audience's connection with celebrities, celetoids and celeactors is dominated by imaginary relationships. The physical and cultural remoteness of the object from the spectator means that audience relationships carry a high propensity of fantasy and desire. The construction of celeactors is often designed to embody stereotypes and prejudices in popular culture. Alf Garnett, Archie Bunker, James Bond, Doug Ross (*ER*), J. R. Ewing, Frasier, Harold and Albert Steptoe, Harry Callahan (*Dirty Harry*), the Fonz, Carrie Bradshaw (*Sex and the City*), Fox Mulder and Dana Scully, to name but a few random celeactors from popular culture over the last 40 years, are imaginary constructions. Nevertheless, although they are imaginary figures involved in fictionalized narratives, they exert tangible and, in some cases, long-term influences over real social relationships and cultural formations. *Inter alia*, they operate as models for emulation, embody desire and galvanize issues in popular culture, dramatize prejudice, affect public opinion and contribute to identity formation. The deaths of the celeactors Inspector Morse and Victor Meldrew, who starred in the popular crime show *Inspector Morse* and the cult BBC TV sit-com *One Foot in the Grave* respectively, occurred within a week of each other. Both deaths were national events, trailed on TV and in the press. The broadcast showing the end of Victor Meldrew was preceded by a 45-minute obituary, an honour usually awarded only to members of the Royal Family.

Of course, the nature of celeactor influence is much debated. Celeactor types have been a major influence in representing 'cool' in post-war culture. In their recent book *Cool Rules*, Dick Pountain and David Robins define 'cool' as 'a *permanent* state of *private* rebellion' that 'conceals its rebellion behind a mask of ironic impassivity'.[5] They maintain that modern cool identity types influence all age groups, and have been a significant influence in post-war culture. The Fonz, Harry Callahan, Doug Ross and Mulder and Scully are obviously celeactors that embody cool. They deal with the complexities and challenges of modern life with insouciant aplomb and efficiency. As such, they offer identity types for appreciation and emulation in popular culture.

Dallas, in contrast, demonstrates the relationship between the stereo-typal roles played by celeactors and the articulation of social criticism and frustrated desire in the audience.[6] The conspicuous consumption and amorality of the Texas tycoons became a way of directing opprobrium against the *nouveaux riches* crudities of the Reagan–Thatcher years. They also provided a dramatized outlet for frustrated wish-fulfilment. Generally, audiences did not regard the Ewing family as role models for emulation. Rather, *Dallas* allowed viewers to vent their disapproval of trends in personality and society without engaging in overtly politicized actions. JR, Bobby and their wives, mistresses and misdemeanours were an escape valve for viewers caught up in the dehumanizing logic of advanced capitalism.

Some of the most influential characters in the genre have emerged from the soap opera format. Celeactors in the worldwide syndicated British soap *Coronation Street*, such as Ena Sharples, Albert Tatlock, Ken Barlow, Bet Lynch, Elsie Tanner, Mike Baldwin, Curly Watts, Jack and Vera Duckworth and Betty Williams, are accepted as 'real' people who embody and reflect the tensions of working-class life in Manchester. *Brookside*, *Emmerdale Farm* and *East Enders* are other examples of successful British soap operas in which celeactors have attained wider influence in popular culture. A notable example in the UK is the character of Grant Mitchell in *East Enders*, played by Ross Kemp. In the 1990s Grant Mitchell was widely perceived by audiences to personify real tensions in British masculinity. His aggression, frustration and pain were held to mirror the challenges posed to traditional masculinity through feminism and the emergence of the casualized labour market.

Soaps have a peculiar capacity to insinuate themselves into popular consciousness. As a staple in the diet of weekly TV broadcasts, they offer rich opportunities to develop narrative and establish an identifiable 'slice of life'. Soap celeactors grow with their audiences, developing nuances of character and incident as the ratings require. The success of comedy shows like *Friends* and *Frasier* reinforce the point. The celeactor characters of Rachel Green, Monica Geller, Phoebe Buffay, Joey Tribbiani and Chandler Bing depicted in *Friends* have achieved phenomenal global appeal. The actors that portray them, namely Jennifer Aniston, Courteney Cox Arquette, Lisa Kudrow, Matt LeBlanc and Matthew Perry, have been so effective in their performances that they are in danger of being typecast. This carries with it a psychological tension for the actor portraying the celeactor: the public face threatens to stifle or suffocate the veridical self.

In this book I have chosen to concentrate primarily on achieved and attributed types of celebrity. This derives from the premise – which I shall attempt to substantiate below – that celebrity only becomes a phenomenon in the age of the common man. Two and a half centuries ago, ascribed celebrity was ascendant. People lived in a relatively fixed society of monarchs, lords and ladies. Court society in pre-Revolutionary France was a *monde* in which bloodline was unequivocally the root of social power and fame. Of course, this society did not exclude achieved celebrity. The international fame acquired by Dante, Michelangelo, Leonardo da Vinci and Shakespeare was not a matter of birth, but of accomplishment. Nor was achieved celebrity confined to the arts. Financiers, merchants, inventors and other self-made men also experienced upward mobility and challenged the boundaries of traditional privilege and prestige. However, within the Ancien Régime they were always under strong pressures to conform to the established procedures and conventions set by the Court.

The French Revolution aimed to sweep away the old order and replace it with universal equality and freedom. It proclaimed the age of the 'new man'. This claim was hardly unique. Cicero had claimed it for himself in Ancient Rome. However, whereas Cicero's claim was an act of self-aggrandizement, in France the Revolution was undertaken with the aim of breaking forever with the tyranny, despotism and hierarchy of the past.

Judged by these exacting standards, the Revolution failed to achieve its objectives. Lineage survived as a source of ascribed status, and under Napoleon's rule many honorific positions based in bloodline were either revived or invented. Napoleon himself adopted the title of 'Emperor' in 1804. Yet it would be a massive over-simplification to infer that the execution of Robespierre and other Revolutionary leaders culminated in the restoration of the Ancien Régime. Robespierre declared a 'republic of virtue', and the metaphor proved to be an enduring and popular image of utopia in the West. Paradoxically, the move to eliminate privilege unintentionally laid the foundations for the emergence of new forms of distinction. Celebrity culture and the celetoid are the direct descendants of the revolt against tyranny. The celeactor is a symptom of the decline of ascribed forms of power and a greater equality in the balance of power between social classes.

Understanding Celebrity: Three Approaches

In positing a close link between social construction and celebrity, I am underscoring the value of an approach to contemporary celebrity that privileges history. This approach has not always been championed in the academic literature on the subject, which is dominated by three contending positions: Subjectivism, Structuralism and Post-structuralism.

SUBJECTIVISM Subjectivist accounts of celebrity fasten on the putative singularity of personal characteristics. In these accounts, celebrity is explained as the reflection of innate talent. Thus, orthodox subjectivism maintains that no one can sing like Caruso, just as no one can replicate Samuel Beckett's dramatic insight into the human condition, emulate Walter Matthau's grumpiness or achieve Kurt Cobain's remarkable artistic angst. Talent is understood to be a unique, ultimately inexplicable phenomenon. While it may be refined and polished through discipline and practice, its singularity is presented as a wonderful gift of nature. Orthodox Subjectivism maintains that the reasons why audiences are intensely affected by the particular gait of a celebrity, the form of face, the manner of reacting and speaking, are matters of unique chemistry. That is, they cannot be rationally explained. Since what confers celebrity status on someone is ultimately regarded to be a mystery, appreciation is privileged over analysis. One should, so to speak, let celebrities 'speak for themselves', and marvel, not meddle, at the reasons for their fame.

Despite this, Subjectivist accounts are not in themselves, so to speak, 'natural'. On the contrary, they reflect a level of human understanding about causality that is achieved by a detachment from both nature and superstition. The first people of singularity in human history were doubtless marked out by their physical or mental power, or, as a sceptic might say, by their capacity to hoodwink others. Perhaps the first coherent audience to bestow distinction on persons regarded as singular projected supernatural powers onto them. Certainly, there is a link between celebrity, religion and magic, a link I shall comment on at greater length in chapter Two.

For the moment, however, consider the case of Alexander the Great. He probably has superior claim to be numbered the first unequivocal *pre-figurative* celebrity in history. The son of Philip, king of the Macedonians, Alexander regarded the ascribed celebrity of monarchial lineage as unduly limiting. He aimed at a higher pretext to explain both his corporeal glory and brave deeds. Through his military triumphs, and his employment of Callisthenes, perhaps the first spin doctor to influence a global audience, Alexander aimed to become a universal, unquestionable 'presence' in everyday life. He sought to inscribe himself on public consciousness as a man apart, a person without precedent. Via the mouthpiece of Callisthenes, Alexander claimed direct descent from the gods of Homeric legend.

The Roman emperors also proclaimed kinship with the Gods. Jupiter, Apollo, Neptune and Mars were the spiritual fathers of Julius Caesar, Mark

Antony, Augustus and other prominent leaders. Yet the distinguishing feature of the Roman tradition of celebrity is the subsumption of individual vanity under the higher authority of the state. Caligula and Nero were notorious figures in Roman culture because they sought personal aggrandizement above their responsibility to the state. In Ancient Rome the celebrity was viewed as the perfect representation of the values of his class and all that was honourable in the imperial capital. Religion and state honour were more enmeshed with politics than they had been in the Alexandrian tradition. The pomp and splendour of the Emperor reflected the might and glory of Rome. Public accountability was implicitly part of celebrity status. By flaunting public accountability, Caligula and Nero invited recrimination.

Here it is perhaps worth making a technical distinction. Notoriety is akin to celebrity in operating through impact on public consciousness. However, whereas celebrity functions within a general moral framework that reaffirms paramount order, notoriety usually connotes transgression, deviance and immorality. Later I will modify this distinction somewhat, for I shall argue that today celebrity often involves transgressing ordinary moral rules by, for example, excessive conspicuous consumption, exhibitionist libidinous gratification, drug abuse, alcohol addiction, violence and so on. As such, a celebrity might be thought of as tapping the surplus material and symbolic value that is inherent in the economic and moral frameworks governing everyday life. On this reckoning, celebrity is, so to speak, the embodiment of surplus, since it radiates greater material and symbolic power than non-celebrity. If the embodiment of surplus means higher status, it also allows for a greater latitude of excessive behaviour. Celebrity is, in fact, often connected with transgression. The fact that celebrities seem to inhabit a different world than the rest of us seems to give them licence to do things we can only dream about.

In both the Alexandrian and the Roman traditions, pre-figurative celebrity status was affirmed and reaffirmed in the public arena. It was associated with exhibitionism, drama, conspicuous consumption and acclaim. The theatre of public life was the stage on which reputations were made and unmade. In ancient society, ostentation, tribute and excess were prominent traits of celebrity culture. Therefore, the exhibitionism that is frequently associated with contemporary celebrity was anticipated in ancient society. One might say that when Britney Spears, Arnold Schwarzenegger, Robbie Williams, Bruce Willis or Caprice cultivate acclaim through public presentation, they affirm that the gods have come down to earth.

Max Weber, a notable critic of unalloyed Subjectivism, none the less devised the concept of charisma to apply to special or unique qualities attributed to the individual.[7] He argued that charismatic authority is, by definition, inspirational. It depends on apparently miraculous or semi-miraculous occurrences, such as prophecies that come true, battles that are always won, powers of healing that never falter, artistic performances that succeed time and again. All these features have overtones in the modern concept of celebrity.

Weber argued that charisma is vested in a person by virtue of popular belief in extraordinary personal qualities. Supernatural forces are often attributed as the cause behind charisma. Perhaps supernatural and theistic explanations of singularity are older than Subjectivist accounts. Faced with a choice between divine inspiration and human fallibility to explain behaviour, one can see why an Alexander, a Cicero or a Nero desired divine kinship. Nor is it the case that supernatural or theistic responses to celebrity have been entirely outmoded. John Lennon complained that disabled people often sought out The Beatles at concerts as divine miracle-workers.

Much of the popular biographical literature on celebrity is based on Subjectivist assumptions. For example, popular chain-store biographies regularly claim that there will never be another John Lennon, that we shall not see the like of Marilyn Monroe again, and that Eva Peron and Princess Diana were matchless in human experience. Pure Subjectivism therefore holds that celebrity is unique. The cultural intermediaries that link a celebrity to an audience are recognized as catalysts in communication. However, the seat of celebrity is the matchless, God-given, creative gifts of the performer.

STRUCTURALISM Unlike Subjectivist accounts, Structuralism concentrates on the interrelations between human conduct and the context that informs conduct. Explanations that assign pronounced significance to putative, singular or unique celebrity qualities are rejected. Instead, celebrity is investigated as the expression of universal structural rules embedded in culture. Broadly speaking, three social structures are usually distinguished in this approach to understanding celebrity: the culture industry, governmentality and type theory.

The culture industry thesis is associated with the Frankfurt School of social criticism. The thesis holds that organized entertainment is a type of social control. The Hollywood machine, Tin Pan Alley and the specialized corporations of the entertainment industry are portrayed as moulders of social conduct. Their ultimate aim is to reinforce and extend the rule of capital. Celebrities are conceptualized as one of the means through which capitalism achieves its ends of subduing and exploiting the masses. They express an ideology of heroic individualism, upward mobility and choice in social conditions wherein standardization, monotony and routine prevail. Thus the identification of the masses with celebrity is always false consciousness, since celebrities are not regarded as reflections of reality, but fabrications designed to enhance the rule of capital.

Capitalism originally sought to police play and pleasure, because any attempt to replace work as the central life interest threatened the economic survival of the system. The family, the state and religion engendered a variety of patterns of moral regulation to control desire and ensure compliance with the system of production. However, as the forces and relations of production developed, consumer culture and leisure time expanded. The principles that operated to repress the individual in the workplace and the home were extended to the shopping mall and recreational activity. The entertainment industry and consumer culture produced what Herbert Marcuse called 'repressive desublimation'.[8] Through this process individuals unconsciously adopted the values of alienated culture, so that they unwittingly subscribed to a degraded version of humanity.

Celebrities appear to enable audiences to gain a sense of release from the privations that beset them in everyday life. However, because of the generalized conditions of alienation that obtain under capitalism, this release can never assume anything other than an estranged and transient form. At the high-water mark of Marcuse's influence in the 1960s, he proposed that repressive desublimation entirely co-opts the power of the masses to resist. He later modified this view, and argued that within the ranks of what might be called 'antinomian' elements in society, notably artists, bohemians, students and the unemployed, a challenge to the rule of capital might be attempted.[9]

A contrasting Leftist tradition argues that capitalism and socialism were merging to create a new system of repression in which celebrity culture mesmerized the masses. For Guy Debord, industrial culture was, above all, a culture of signs.[10] The purpose of celebrity culture is to shepherd the populace into imitative consumption. A system organized around the semiotics of control eventually eliminates the requirement for physical repression. Domination is universal, and operates through signs of achieved celebrity and the society of the spectacle. But this account has been heavily criticized for being over-fatalistic. It identifies no escape from the domination of celebrity and the spectacle. Indeed, this position was corrosively dismissive of contemporary counter-culture on the grounds that it would inevitably be absorbed by celebrity culture.

By and large, according to Edgar Morin, celebrities do fulfil the functions required of them by entertainment moguls.[11] In this sense they are the servants of capital. Nothing illustrates this more starkly than the tendency of the entertainment industry to drop celebrities once their grip on the public is judged to have diminished. Kenneth Anger's inventory of the suicides, crack-ups and narcotic addictions of downwardly mobile Hollywood stars between the 1920s and '80s offers cautionary data.[12] Our own day has witnessed the examples of public humiliation and career decline suffered by O. J. Simpson and Gary Glitter following revelations about their unsavoury private lives and the highly publicized court cases that accompanied them.

Morin's work is significant for subverting the proposition that celebrities are created by the culture industry. According to him, celebrity impresarios do not create celebrity appeal. Nor is this appeal to be explained in terms of the innate talent of the celebrity. Instead, Morin favours an explanation of celebrity that explores celebrity power as a projection of the pent-up needs of the audience. On this reckoning, celebrities are akin to transformers, accumulating and enlarging the dehumanized desires of the audience, and momentarily rehumanizing them through dramatized public representation and release. Morin therefore overturns the Frankfurt School's emphasis on the dominant class as the motive force behind celebrity appeal. In its place he holds that we are attracted to celebrities because they are presented as the antithesis of a generalized psychological lack in ourselves.

For Morin and others, life relations under capitalism constitute an illusory state of affairs. That is, ideology and commodification operate to mask and corrupt human nature by alienating person from person. It is because capitalism estranges us so thoroughly from one another, and from our own natures, that we project our fantasies of belonging and fulfilment onto celebrities, i.e., idealized forms of the self that is routinely degraded in commodity culture. As for the autonomy of the celebrity – that autonomy is always imaginary. True, for the Frankfurt School celebrity is presented as the conducting rod of dominant power, whereas for Morin it is the expression of the frustrated desires of the audience. Yet, in both, the celebrity is finally analyzed as the embodiment of ideology.

Marcuse, Debord, Morin and other writers are critical of many features of Marxian theory, but they remain loyal to Marxian concepts of ideology, class and transcendence. This is not true of those approaches in Structuralism that view celebrity through the prism of governmentality. Whether explicitly expressed or not, the decisive influence here has been Michel Foucault. His contribution to the question of governmentality can be stated quite precisely. The Marxian tradition favoured the metaphor of enveloping canopies of oppression and control over individual behaviour; class, alienation, ideology, commodification are just some examples that come to mind. Against this, Foucault's application of governmentality emphasizes *régimes* of control and fragmentation of order. He argued that social order is produced by discourses of power.[13] A discourse may be thought of as consisting of a distinctive rhetorical language, associated symbolic capital and rules of practice, and a template of social realism, which establishes some forms of behaviour as relevant and authentic and casts others as insignificant and trivial.

Discourses are the means through which regimes of power are enunciated. For example, the New Right's proposition, developed in the 1980s and '90s, that there is 'no alternative' to market organization, prioritized one form of ontology (the theory of being) and epistemology (the theory of science or criteria of knowledge) and sought to consign others to the dustbin of history. Note that discourses do not rely primarily on physical power to achieve their effect. Rather, they deploy symbolic devices and rhetoric to achieve their hold over social practice. Further, since order is conceived as a regime of power in which varieties of specialized discourse co-exist in a state of perpetual tension with each other, Foucault recognized a provisional quality to social and cultural reproduction. Discourses are challenged, and discourses resist. Thus, governmentality is always a question of action and reaction, in which social forces are located and reconfigured in strategic combinations.

Within the study of celebrity, this approach has been most fully developed by David Marshall who argues that celebrity has a political function.[14]

It operates to articulate, and legitimate, various forms of subjectivity that enhance the value of individuality and personality. Through these means, order and compliance are reproduced. For example, the pre-eminence enjoyed by sports celebrities, such as Pete Sampras, Magic Johnson, Martina Hingis, Lindsay Davenport, Tiger Woods, Michael Owen and David Beckham, underlines the connection between self-discipline, training and material success as 'examples to us all'. These sports celebrities are typically portrayed as superlatively talented and hard-working individuals who contribute to the pre-eminence of the dual ethic of individualism and personal competitiveness in society. At the same time, the emphasis on luck in celebrity sporting achievement encourages the masses to adopt a fatalistic attitude to life, rather than to question the distributive logic of a system that allocates life chances so unequally.

Movie plots starring celebrities are caught up in the same general process. Tom Cruise in *Top Gun* (1986), Harrison Ford in the *Indiana Jones* and *Star Wars* series, Liam Neeson in *Schindler's List* (1993), Bruce Willis in the *Die Hard* series, Mel Gibson in the *Lethal Weapon* series and Tom Hanks in *Forrest Gump* (1994) essentially enact morality tales in which good triumphs over evil, merit is rewarded and justice prevails.

Marshall argues that celebrity is emphatically a social construction, in which the mass-media play a leading role in governing the population. Government is accomplished by providing suitable role models, morality tales that either reconcile ordinary people to their subordination or provide escapism from the hardships of life. However, he wishes to incorporate the notion of the audience as productive agents in developing the meaning of celebrity. To this end he introduces the term 'audience-subjectivities' to refer to the constant negotiation around the public face of celebrity, between types or forms of audience and particular cultural industries. Marshall's shift is intended both to deflect analysis from attributing omnipotence to the mass-media and to propose that audiences must be regarded as sophisticated, creative agents in the construction and development of the celebrity system.

Marshall's account links the emergence of the celebrity system to the main problem of governmentality in the nineteenth and twentieth centuries, namely control of the crowd. Citing the classical works on urban policing by Gabriel Tarde and Gustave Le Bon,[15] Marshall argues that the concentration of populations in urban–industrial settings inevitably produced public anxieties about the possibilities of civil disobedience and social disorder. Both Tarde and Le Bon developed a social psychology of crowd behaviour that was a seminal influence on law and order policy. One facet of their work was to recognize the value of symbolic power in regulating mass behaviour. Psychoanalytical method, which emerged at roughly the same time, reinforced this by assigning a pronounced significance to symbols, signs and metaphors in the conduct of social life. Marshall connects the celebrity system with the origins of governing urban–industrial populations. He contends that 'celebrities are *attempts* to contain the mass' (emphasis in the original).[16] They do so principally by symbolic means. That is, they present preferred models of subjectivity with which audiences are encouraged to identify. They are, so to speak, 'the star police' of modern democracies. In other words, they radiate glamour and attraction, and, in their achieved form, they automatically demonstrate that the system rewards talent and cherishes upward mobility.

Marshall does not discount the proposal that celebrities have transformational power. On the contrary, by identifying achieved celebrities as men and women 'of the people' who have dramatically made good, he acknowledges a critical capacity in celebrity power. For example, Noel and Liam Gallagher have the capacity to criticize the discursive regimes that subordinate the masses, just as Lennon, McCartney, Dylan and Townshend did in the 1960s and The Clash, The Sex Pistols and The Jam did in the 1970s and '80s. However, in privileging the containing role of celebrity power, Marshall indicates that co-option into established regimes of power is the orthodox course of events. In other words, his analysis predicts that the fate of young radicals is to become figureheads of the establishment, and that audiences are finally docile and obedient.

An interesting parallel can be found in Peter Biskind's study of the rise of the *auteur* director in Hollywood in the 1960s and '70s.[17] He describes how directors like Peter Bogdanovitch, Francis Coppola, Stanley Kubrick, Dennis Hopper, Mike Nichols and, later, Martin Scorsese, Stephen Spielberg, Paul Schrader, Brian De Palma and Terence Malick emerged to break the studio system. In the Golden Age of this system, roughly between the late 1920s and the end of the '50s, the producer was king. Moguls like David Selznick, Jack Warner, Louis B. Mayer and Sam Goldwyn presided ruthlessly over the industry, making and breaking stars, cutting scripts unilaterally and firing directors who resisted. Their power turned them into celebrities in their own right, feared by the Hollywood intelligentsia and recognized by the public as the true pharaohs of film. For a while the *auteurs* succeeded in overturning this system by producing unorthodox, counter cultural box-office hits like *Easy Rider, Bonnie & Clyde, The Last Picture Show* and *Chinatown*. Biskind's absorbing account reveals how the grandiose hopes of some of the leading *auteurs*, and bickering and in-fighting among their ranks, gradually culminated in the renaissance of corporate studio power in the 1990s. A new generation of producers, including Don Simpson, Jerry Bruckheimer, Michael Eisner, Joe Roth and Barry Diller, became ascendant, and entertainment corporations like Disney, Sony and Dreamworks now bankrolled and shaped movies.

What Biskind has described is in actuality a classical process of celebrity co-option, in which the independence of the leading *auteur* directors and stars is slowly redefined and reabsorbed by the established regime. This is not to say that new entertainment corporations in Hollywood simply reprise the Golden Age of the Hollywood mogul. Biskind is concerned to show that the new regime of power has learned from the innovations and success of the *auteurs* in creating novel audience subjectivities. However, in doing so he ultimately confirms Marshall's proposition that co-option to corporate control is the dominant, long-term tendency in market society.

Joshua Gamson's work broadly confirms Marshall's connection between celebrity and governmentality, but without the latter's rather jaundiced political sensibility. Gamson's is, in fact, a quintessentially liberal, progressive reading of celebrity. While he recognizes that processes of manipulation, mystification, artificiality and control are integral to the celebrity system, he maintains that 'when audiences play with celebrity, they are playing with the dilemmas of democratic power'.[18] Show business is thus presented not only as a mirror of commercial culture but as part of the pedagogy of citizenship. By studying show people, the citizen understands more about how the entire system works, or could work, in a redeemed world.

This is not an objectionable position, but arguably it is a facile one. The questions are: How does the celebrity system educate the masses? Why do some forms of artifice persuade, and others fail? What kind of ambivalence does the celebrity system make transparent, and what types does it occlude? To be fair, Gamson touches on all of these questions. The difficulty is that he never seizes on any of them in a coherent, solid or consistently critical way. Even so, his observation that the conventions of celebrity collude with those of party politics is a stimulating one. Political success requires that leaders like Bill Clinton, George W. Bush and Tony Blair must play at being their public face. When this goes wrong, as it did catastrophically with Clinton in the Monica Lewinsky affair, it raises damaging questions about both the veridical self and the public face.

The third variant of Structuralism postulates that celebrity is the extension of what might be called foundational types of character and embodiment in society. According to Orrin Klapp, all social groups devise character types that function as role models of leadership.[19] In antiquity the gods laid down mythical narratives and criteria against which concrete instances of human character and behaviour were evaluated. Many of the role models and behavioural standards of antiquity continue to shape our perceptions of courage, nobility, wisdom, beauty and integrity. Hence, the heroic, gallant masculine role cultivated by Hollywood film stars like John Wayne, Harrison Ford, Kevin Costner, Mel Gibson and Clint Eastwood draw on these models and standards.

Klapp does not postulate ancient roots for contemporary foundational categories. Indeed, a significant weakness of his argument is the absence of a tenable historical dimension. Thus, his account provides no explanation of the origins of social types and no discussion of the historical variations in their composition and influence. Instead, he confines his task to an analysis of the primary foundational types in contemporary society, the popularity of which he relates to the success of the mass communications industry. Among the social types he identifies are the hero, the good Joe, the villain, the tough guy, the snob, the prude and the love queen. Celebrities are theorized as the personifications of these foundational types. In Klapp's reading of 1960s America, Perry Como, Bob Hope, Lucille Ball, Bing Crosby and William Holden represent the good Joe; Zsa Zsa Gabor, Grace Kelly and Katherine Hepburn embody the snob; Ernest Hemingway and celeactors like the film gangster Little Caesar and Mickey Spillane's Mike Hammer incarnate the tough guy; while Marilyn Monroe and Ava Gardner are personifications of the love queen. Klapp argues that the celebrity system provides important sources of cultural leadership, social emulation and psychological reinforcement.

Although he does not make the connection, there are parallels to be drawn between Klapp's work and the sociology of Erving Goffman.[20] Goffman applies a dramaturgical approach to the analysis of everyday life. Interaction is explored in terms of 'scripts', 'roles' and 'performances'. On this account, celebrity may be read as a concentrated, idealized form of generalized traits or aspirations of embodiment and character. However, Goffman's approach is more successful in demonstrating how presentation is manipulated and mythologized by economic and cultural forces in order to manufacture social impact. In contrast, Klapp's version of foundational type theory inclines towards a naturalistic approach in explaining celebrity. Although celebrity is presented as the reflection of foundational social types, the operation of economic, cultural and political power in the construction of celebrity is a missing dimension in his work, and this severely limits its use. It also fails to tackle the growth of notoriety and sensationalism in the celebrity race, which, I maintain, is a paramount feature in the celebrification process today.

The popularity of screen idols in the 1920s, such as John Barrymore, Douglas Fairbanks and Rudolph Valentino, has also been explained in Structuralist terms. That is, they are regarded as constructed responses to the crisis in masculine identity wrought by the liberation of women and economic uncertainty. Gaylyn Studlar's central proposition is that the established, normative constructs of masculinity were decomposing in the 1920s.[21] The media of the day were obsessed by worries that the greater public presence and power of women in society would create 'woman-made masculinity'. This was associated with epicene, physically passive characteristics. Traditional ideals of masculinity were under intense pressure, and men were confused about their new role in post-patriarchal culture. In this cultural context, masculine celebrity identities in the 1920s can be interpreted as calculated cultural reactions to a perceived crisis in sexual politics. Thus, the popularity of Douglas Fairbanks is explained as a retreat into the escapism of childhood romanticism that reaffirmed the 'natural' masculine values of adventure and action. Barrymore and Valentino were idealized versions of super-heroes, gloriously free of the sexual and economic anxieties that encumbered the audience. In contrast, Valentino's calculated 'foreign' exoticism challenged cinemagoers by insinuating effeminacy in the character of the American male. The celebrity construct developed by the actor Lon Chaney is perhaps an interesting variant in this analysis. The estranged, bitter, grotesque characters that became Chaney's trademark might be read as radical negations of the escapist, idealized types of masculinity represented by Fairbanks, Barrymore and Valentino, and, by extension, American consumer culture. Chaney's roles testify to the mutilation of the ideal of normative masculinity and dramatize the alienation of the audience from both idealized role models and the everyday anxieties of sexual politics.

Structuralist approaches to celebrity were highly influential between the 1960s and '80s. They appeared to offer the prospect of a scientific understanding of celebrity, and they avoided the naturalistic fallacies of subjectivism. Instead, the aetiology of celebrity was explained in terms of determinate, totalizing structures of influence: the culture industry, capitalism, masculinity. It would be unwise to minimize the rhetorical power of these explanations compared to the accounts offered by fanzines, authorized biographies or self-reporting by celebrities. On the other hand, Structuralists rarely took the trouble to test their propositions empirically. In many cases, this exaggerated the importance of the designated structure of social control and neutralized the knowledge, skills and power of social actors to resist. For example, in the strongest versions of the culture industry thesis, celebrity is explained as a triumph of the manipulative influence of entertainment moguls, PR specialists and image makers. The knowledge, desire and judgement of the audience are sidelined.

Structuralist accounts also possess a tendency to exaggerate the uniformity of structural forces. The cultural capital of the entertainment industry, and the state apparatus, does not resemble a uniform and undifferentiated whole. Rather, it is more accurate to view it in terms of taste cultures, cleavages and contingent, negotiated settlements. By viewing structural influence in this way, a more compelling analysis emerges of social change and the politics of celebrity management.

POST-STRUCTURALISM Instead of focusing on the relationship between concrete celebrities and the historical structure behind them, Post-structuralist accounts concentrate on the omnipresent celebrity image and the codes of representation through which this image is reproduced, developed and consumed. Richard Dyer is probably the principal exponent of this approach, someone for whom 'stars represent typical ways of behaving, feeling and thinking in contemporary society'.[22] This appears to follow the argument that celebrities are the representation of foundational types of character and embodiment, but Dyer is convinced that foundational types must always be examined in relation to historical, cultural and socio-economic contexts. There is, then, an interplay between the narrative of celebrity and the historical, cultural and socio-economic contexts to which celebrity is attached. To use a term from Post-structuralism, celebrity is 'inter-textually' constructed and developed.

Contra Structuralism and Subjectivism, Dyer maintains that neither structural determinism nor 'the raw material of the person' are sufficient explanations of achieved celebrity. Rather, the psychology and body of the person constitute a set of resources that have to be polished and refined by the mass-media – the agencies of the culture industry charged with the task of designing celebrities for public consumption.

Superficially, this may be taken to confirm the culture industry thesis, since it appears to posit that the producers who manage and present a celebrity to the public have ultimate power. However, central to the Post-structuralist approach is the notion that star images are inflected and modified by the mass-media and the productive assimilation of the audience. Thus a dispersed view of power is articulated in which celebrity is examined as a developing field of intertextual representation in which meaning is variously assembled. Variation derives from the different constructions and inflections vested in the celebrity by the participants in the field, including agents, press officers, gossip columnists, producers and fans.

Richard deCordova also argued for an inter-textual approach to stardom.[23] The meaning of stars is organized by their repertory of films, and by publicity in the form of biographies, autobiographies, interviews, critical studies, newspaper articles and fan responses. For deCordova these aspects of stardom are an essential part of the production and consumption of celebrity. Simultaneously, then, Post-structuralism both centres consciousness on the performer and decentres that consciousness by relating the presence and meaning of celebrity to a developing field of interests.

Post-structuralist approaches therefore treat notions of the individual and individualization as inherently problematic. By addressing celebrity as a field of production, representation and consumption, they move away from Subjectivist accounts that prioritize the meaning of celebrity in the character, talent and embodiment of the subject. Similarly, by pursuing celebrity as the emerging property of interactions in a determinate field of interests, Post-structuralism transcends the problems of monolithic, static analysis frequently associated with Structuralism. Dyer's analysis of the iconic status of Judy Garland in the gay community illustrates the processes of inflection and reappropriation in the consumption of the celebrity image.[24] The public face of Garland as a bruised, battered, misunderstood talent suggested parallels with gay and lesbian experience in articulating identity and desire. This public face, which in many ways invalidated the image of Dorothy in *The Wizard of Oz* that Garland cultivated as a child star, emerged from the resonance her personal problems had with a considerable element in her fan base, and the calculations of her managers, publicists and career advisers. Above all, the Post-structuralist approach confirms the importance of understanding celebrity as a developing, relational field of power, and it emphasizes the versatility and contradictions of the public face.

Surface Relations and Celebrity Involvement Shields

All three dominant approaches in the study of celebrity emphasize the centrality of the mass-media, and with good reason. The relationship between celebrities and fans is typically mediated through representation. As we have seen, out-of-face encounters may conflict with how fans regard the public face of the celebrity. However, despite the increasing profusion of celebrities in society, such encounters are comparatively rare. The mass-media constitute the prime channel of contact between fans and celebrities. Stage, screen, audio transmission and print culture are the main institutional mechanisms that express the various idioms of celebrity culture. Each presupposes distance between the celebrity and the audience. Celebrity culture is, in fact, overwhelmingly a culture of surface relations.

With respect to the relation of the celebrity to the fan, celebrities usually develop what Goffman called 'involvement shields', which hide the veridical self from the public face. These 'shields' can be raised when celebrities attend conventions, public celebrations or other ceremonies held in their honour. Notwithstanding this, the general attitude celebrities cultivate in relation to their fans is that of negotiating with an abstract other. This attitude necessarily predisposes unfocused physical encounters between the celebrity and the fan to be conducted on a surface level, since the celebrity's veridical self is concealed on *a priori* grounds. By 'unfocused physical encounters' I mean chance contacts, in which the celebrity has been unable to prepare and polish a tenable public face for a scripted occasion. In these circumstances, mediation between the veridical self and the audience is, perhaps understandably, apt to be one-sided, glancing and unsatisfactory. This is not to say that Uma Thurman, Matt Damon or Tony Blair will be anything other than civil to you if you bump into them on the street. But it perhaps reinforces the common-sense presupposition that the idiom of such encounters rarely permits them to go deeper than surface pleasantries.

What of the relation of the fan to the celebrity? Here reciprocal relations are constructed around an anonymous consumer and a public face.

The boundaries of attachment between the public face and the fan are not clearly delineated. Consuming celebrity products, and generally reinforcing the image of the public face in ordinary social interaction, are merely the outward manifestations of attachment. At deeper psychic levels, fans may adopt the values and style of the public face and, in some cases, develop unmanageable obsessions. This is particularly likely where fans are isolated or detached from significant others in family and kinship networks. Isolation may produce over-identification with the public face and engender the desire to possess the celebrity or deprive the public face of volition. I examine stalking and celebrity in chapter Four. Here, it is perhaps worth noting that, in 1990 Rebecca Schaeffer, the star of the sitcom *My Sister Sam*, was murdered by an obsessive fan who forced his way into her home. In 1999 Jill Dando, the popular BBC TV presenter, was shot dead on her own doorstep by a stalker. These violent acts point to the strength of the fantasies and obsessions that some fans nurture for celebrity figures.

These fantasies and obsessions may turn inward, so that when a celebrity dies the fan decides that his or her own life is no longer worth living. Following the deaths of Rudolph Valentino, Elvis Presley, Kurt Cobain and John Lennon, some suicides were reported.

The audience responds to the celebrity through abstract desire. This desire is alienable in as much as it switches in response to commodity and brand innovation. This is particularly evident in youth culture. The history of Pop music is littered with has-been teenybop sensations: Sweet, The Bay City Rollers and David Cassidy from the '70s; Bros, Adam Ant and Andrew Ridgeley from the '80s; Chesney Hawkes, Kriss Kross and Vanilla Ice from the '90s. It is also evident in the cases of suicide that accompany the death of a major celebrity. Here the desire of the fan overwhelms personal well-being. Abstract desire is the only reason to live, and when the referent of this desire – the celebrity – dies, life for the fan becomes meaningless. This radical division between abstract desire and embodied well-being is also evident in examples of fan self-mutilation, drug dependency and alcohol abuse, in which the fan seeks to negate the pain of unconsummated desire.

These examples suggest that there is considerable fuzziness between the public face of celebrity and fandom. Further, fandom can be as frustrating as it is exhilarating, and psychically damaging rather than fulfilling. However, the psychic attachment that a fan develops for a celebrity seldom culminates in physical attack, murder or suicide. Even so, psychic attachments may be a significant element in identity formation and the ordering of personal and subcultural history.

Research into collective memory and the British royal family has found that royal events like births, marriages and deaths provided frames for the recollection of personal experience. Identity formation in this case is not necessarily founded in the introjection of the values and style of the public face. People may be openly cynical about the royal family, and mock their gravitas and apparent innate sense of superiority. Role distance is built into the majority of fan relations with celebrities. The popular notion of the adoring audience has limitations, and fans are capable of withdrawing attachment as well as affirming it. None the less, it remains culturally significant that collective memory is influenced by celebrity history, so that *temps perdu* in personal biography are recalled by reference to external events in celebrity history.

The surface character of celebrity culture is oddly illuminating. Other than religion, celebrity culture is the only cluster of human relationships in which mutual passion typically operates without physical interaction. The general form of interaction between the fan and the celebrity takes the form of the consumer absorbing a mediated image. Similarly, celebrities may meet fans at conventions and public events or through out-of-face encounters, but they typically relate to fans as an abstraction, which is also translated through the mass-media rather than direct or prolonged face-to-face interaction.

It may seem beside the point to compare celebrity with religion.

Religion, after all, refers to the formulation of belief in a general order of existence, in which powerful, durable attachments are invested in spiritually relevant objects or persons. A famous strand within academic study holds that religious belief is based on a dichotomy between the sacred and the profane. Objects and persons belonging to the sacred level are conceptualized as spiritual entities possessing purity and power that contrasts with the profane level of mortal life. Some celebrities have indeed laid claim to sacred and spiritual qualities. Napoleon and Hitler were worshipped in their day as saviours of their respective nations. But the belief invested in them was conditional. They exemplified the form of charisma, identified by Max Weber, in which faith derives from a belief in extraordinary attributes. When Napoleon and Hitler began to suffer military setbacks, their charismatic status waned. In any case, the charisma of these figures never approached the general, unconditional faith that is the primary quality of Christianity and Islam.

There is much, then, to caution against over-zealous comparisons between celebrity and religion. None the less, Christianity is adopting many of the devices of consumer culture in branding belief and communicating faith. Thus, religious crusades have been held in Disneyland, with Christian artists performing on stages and salvationists preaching the gospel message. Email websites have been constructed to promote e-spirituality. Religious belief is being reconfigured to provide meaning and solidarity as responses to the uprooting effect of globalization. Because these responses are communicated through the mass-media, they borrow the style and form of celebrity culture. We need to examine whether there has been a partial or total convergence between celebrity culture and religion.

CHAPTER TWO

Celebrity and Religion

Celebrity worship is regularly condemned in public as idolatry, which carries connotations of slavery, false consciousness and 'the Devil's work'. More prosaically, it is bracketed with triviality and superficiality. Certainly, relationships between fans and celebrities frequently involve unusually high levels of non-reciprocal emotional dependence, in which fans project intensely positive feelings onto the celebrity. The obsessed fan participates in imaginary relations of intimacy with the celebrity. In extreme cases these relations may be a substitute for the real relations of marriage, family and work. For example, Fred and Judy Vermorel,[1] who interviewed many fans in order to question them about the reasons and motives behind their devotion, reported that Joanne, a middle-aged Barry Manilow fan with three children, admitted that when she made love with her husband she imagined him to be Barry. She compared her devotion to Barry with religious experience, in as much as it provided a grounded, affirming quality to her life. Other respondents declared that they regularly engaged in mind-voyaging or mild fantasy-work with the celebrity as the precious other. That is, streams-of-identity thought that imaginatively projected them into the experience of the celebrity to whom they found themselves attracted. High levels of identification are reflected in the wardrobe, vocabulary and leisure practice of such fans. In rare cases they undergo cosmetic surgery to acquire a simulacrum of the celebrity's public face. More generally, the celebrity is an imaginary resource to turn to in the midst of life's hardships or triumphs, to gain solace from, to beseech for wisdom and joy. Piquantly, one ventures that hatred is never far from the surface of adulation because the fan's desire for consummation is doomed to fail.

For fans like Joanne, the emotions aroused by the celebrity do not belong to the levels of trivial or superficial experience. Nor do they belong to the categories of slavery or false consciousness, as some Structuralist accounts suggest. On the contrary, these fans seek validation in imaginary relationships with the celebrity to whom they are attached in order to compensate for feelings of invalidation and incompleteness elsewhere in their lives. It is as if the celebrity provides a path into genuine meaningful experience, and the routine order of domesticity and work is the domain of inauthenticity.

The term 'para-social interaction' is used to refer to relations of intimacy constructed through the mass-media rather than direct experience and face-to-face meetings. This is a form of second-order intimacy, since it derives from representations of the person rather than actual physical contact. None the less, in societies in which as many as 50 per cent of the population confess to sub-clinical feelings of isolation and loneliness, para-social interaction is a significant aspect of the search for recognition and belonging. Celebrities offer peculiarly powerful affirmations of belonging, recognition and meaning in the midst of the lives of their audiences, lives that may otherwise be poignantly experienced as under-performing, anti-climactic or sub-clinically depressing. A peculiar tension in celebrity culture is that the physical and social remoteness of the celebrity is compensated for by the glut of mass-media information, including fanzines, press stories, TV documentaries, interviews, newsletters and biographies, which personalize the celebrity, turning a distant figure from a stranger into a significant other. The tension has inescapable parallels with religious worship, and these are reinforced by the attribution by fans of magical or extraordinary powers to the celebrity. Celebrities are thought to possess God-like qualities by some fans, while others – experiencing the power of the celebrity to arouse deep emotions – recognize the spirit of the shaman.

Shamanism and Celebrity

Anthropological studies of comparative religion and shamanism demonstrate that all cultures possess rites, myths, divine forms, sacred and venerated objects, symbols, consecrated men and sacred places. Each category is attached to a distinctive morphology that organizes experience and bestows sacred or extraordinary meaning on certain types of conduct and experience. It is reasonable to think of these morphologies as establishing principles of inclusion and exclusion. Indeed, all religious systems are ultimately founded on these principles. In secular society, the sacred loses its connotation with organized religious belief and becomes attached to mass-media celebrities who become objects of cult worship. Magic is often associated with celebrities, and powers of healing and second sight are frequently attributed to them. Rock concerts can generate ecstasy and swooning in the audience, which is comparable to some rites of magic.

In order to contextualize the link between shamanism and celebrity, which will be substantiated later, it is necessary to say a little more about the nature of the sacred and the history of magic. At the outset, one should be aware that there is huge diversity in the content of sacred morphologies. Yet they also share significant common structural features. These are generally expressed as the manifestation of the sacred in a material fragment of the universe. This manifestation may either be personalized, in the form of a particular human being, or depersonalized, in the form of a physical object or cultural artefact, such as a river, a rock formation or a stone circle. In either case, it is the focus of intense, and occasionally over-powering, feelings of recognition, awe and wonder.

Keith Thomas's detailed account of the history of magic in England traces a long decline from the high point in the Middle Ages, when ecstatic and healing powers were widely attributed to sorcerers, witches and wizards.[2] Urban–industrial development and the rise of science combined to prune back these folk beliefs. However, neither the Puritan nor Scientific Revolutions succeeded in completely uprooting them. The popularity of Spiritualist and New Age beliefs today reveals the strength of the sentiment of anti-scientism and the persistence of folk beliefs in magic and the sacred. If organized religion has declined, it is counterbalanced by the tenacity of strong spiritualist beliefs in Nature and the indivisible struggle in the world between good and evil.

According to the anthropologist Mircea Eliade, nearly all religions posit the existence of sky gods or celestial beings.[3] Human experience is typically divided into three realms: sky, earth and underworld. Men and women are of the earth, but their lives are invested with heightened meaning by the journeys – offered through religious rites and ceremonies – to the sky or the underworld. Most religions can be structurally reduced to a combination of rites and ceremonies of ascent and descent. Journeys above and below are associated with ecstatic experience.

To some extent, this form of ecstasy can be explained as a function, per se, of transgression – that is, conscious desire and behaviour that breaks moral and social conventions. Transgression is a universal characteristic of human culture. It is a source of anxiety and curiosity, prohibition and pleasure. The journey to the sky or underworld is inherently transgressive, because it involves entering realms that are seldom visible in earthly life. By penetrating the veil of prohibitions, religious rites and ceremonies, individuals satisfy their curiosity and experience ecstasy. The journey has a different purpose. Entry to the underworld allows contact with the dead, who, theoretically, possess all knowledge. The journey to the sky brings one closer to the eternal knowledge of the divinities that rule the earth. The journeys provide one with knowledge that cannot be gained by earthly delving or reflection. The underworld is a realm of past knowledge that can illuminate the conditions of the present.

Shamans, sorcerers and medicine men are distinguished by extraordinary qualities. All have been singled out by the spirits, either by virtue of bloodline, or by dint of stigmata. The stigmata may be physical, such as ugliness and deformity, or neuro-psychological, such as a nervous disorder or neurological disability. Shamans, sorcerers and medicine men are believed to possess what, in the Melanesian belief system, is called *mana* – the mysterious, active power that belongs to some living people, and which is shared by the souls of the dead and all spirits. *Mana* enables individuals to conduct rites of worship that assist journeys to sky and underworld.

Ascension rites typically involve a sacrifice, usually of an animal. The sacrifice frees the soul of the slaughtered being and the shaman accompanies the soul on its journey to the sky. Ascension rites also usually involve physical acts of climbing – up mountains, for example, or trees. Rites of descent require the shaman to become like the dead, generally through fasting or symbolic burial, which reveals the sub-frame of the body, but also by forms of self-mutilation, such as burning or cutting.

Religious rites typically involve the wearing of masks that announce the incarnation of a spirit (ancestor, mythical animal or god). The shamanic seance is constructed around spectacle and the interruption of patterned routine. Magical feats, such as rope- and fire-tricks, the consumption of drugs and alcohol, and the relaxation of conventional mores of dress and deportment, disrupt the collective sense of earthly order. In Eliade's words:

The exhibition of magical feats reveals another world – the fabulous world of the gods and magicians, the world in which *everything seems possible*, where the dead return to life and the living die only to live again, where one can disappear and reappear instantaneously, where the 'laws of nature' are abolished, and a certain superhuman 'freedom' is exemplified and made dazzlingly *present* ... the shamanic 'miracles' not only confirm and reinforce the patterns of the traditional religion, they also stimulate and feed the imagination, demolish the barriers between dream and present reality, open windows upon worlds, inhabited by the gods, the dead, and the spirits.[4]

The shamanic spectacle is associated with revelation and rebirth. The ostensible purpose of the spectacle is to achieve social reintegration. The shaman stands out in the tribe as a figure who possesses the capacity for transgression. This is because the shaman possesses the power to conjure different collective intensities of being that, through the metaphor and experience of the ecstatic journey, admit transcendence.

Religion, Collective Effervescence and Celebrity

Might we postulate a connection between celebrity culture and religion? After all, in his classical study of religion, Emile Durkheim, anticipating later anthropological findings, proposed that the religious ceremony both consecrates the sacred belief system of the community and provides an outlet for 'collective effervescence'.[5] The latter condition refers to a state of popular excitement, frenzy, even ecstasy. Durkheim argued that the growth of moral individualism is bound to reduce the significance of organized religion. However, since social equilibrium demands structured breaks from routine, the state must assume responsibility for organizing a series of regular secular holidays in which collective effervescence can be released and the bonds of collective life reaffirmed.

Durkheim's prediction about the decline in popularity of organized religion has proved to be accurate. However, his proposition that state policy should increase the number of secular holidays never came to pass. To be sure, secular holidays increased in the twentieth century, but they rarely adopted the programmatic form of organized collective effervescence. With notable exceptions, such as New Year's Eve celebrations, Bastille Day, Mardi Gras and so forth, days off have tended to be interpreted as time spent with partners and kids, rather than as opportunities for remaking a moral life with others.

The secularization thesis usefully draws attention to the deregulation and de-institutionalization of religion. However, it exaggerates the degree to which religion has been replaced by science and legal–rational systems of thought. Religious belief has certainly been partly restructured around nature and culture. For example, spectator sports, the animal rights campaign and various ecological movements clearly arouse intense collective effervescence that has religious qualities. That is, they replicate clear principles of inclusion and exclusion, they are faithful to transcendent spiritual beliefs and principles, and they identify sacred and profane values. There appears, then, to have been substantial convergence between religion and consumer culture. For our purposes, the decisive question is the degree of convergence.

Neal Gabler posits a 'moral equivalence' between the dedication to God and the worship of celebrity.[6] In doing so, he suggests that celebrity culture is secular society's rejoinder to the decline of religion and magic. Celebrity culture is now ubiquitous, and establishes the main scripts, presentational props, conversational codes and other source materials through which cultural relations are constructed. Gabler's account suggests not so much a convergence between consumer culture and religion as a one-way takeover, in which commodities and celebrity culture emerge as the lynchpins of belonging, recognition and spiritual life. Does this view stand up?

Theologians submit that religion is our 'ultimate concern'. By this is meant that religion addresses the fundamental questions of being in the world. Even if traditional organized religion declines, these questions do not disappear. Since the 1960s, the revival of Spiritualism and New Age cultism suggests that these questions remain prominent in culture. But the growing significance of celebrity culture as, so to speak, the backcloth of routine existence reinforces the proposition that, as it were, 'post-God' celebrity is now one of the mainstays of organizing recognition and belonging in secular society.

Celebrity Reliquaries and Death Rites

There are many striking parallels between religious belief and practice and celebrity cultures that reinforce the hypothesis that considerable partial convergence between religion and celebrity has occurred. In secular society fans build their own reliquaries of celebrity culture. Always, the organizing principle behind the reliquary, from the standpoint of the fan, is to diminish the distance between the fan and the celebrity. From Hollywood's earliest days there are reports of fans requesting film stars' soap, a chewed piece of gum, cigarette butts, lipstick tissues and even a blade of grass from a star's lawn. One wonders how many unrecorded incidents there are of individuals sifting through celebrity dustbins in search of a discarded accessory of fame.

Anthropologists observe that ancestor worship and cults organized around the dead are prominent features of shamanism in Asia and Africa. Relics of the dead often form a part of rites of initiation and worship. The Melanesians believe that a dead man's bone possesses *mana* because the spirit inheres in the bone. They also believe that the excretions of the shaman are receptacles of power because they externalize embodied *mana*.

Christians also believe that the blood, sweat, hair and semen of the saints possess healing powers. The preservation of relics from the bodies and possessions of the saints is a common feature of religious practice.

In secular society, celebrity reliquaries range from items from public sales of Andy Warhol's collection of junk to Jacqueline Kennedy's possessions and Princess Diana's dresses. All fetched astounding prices. Swatch watches collected by Warhol that cost $40 were sold for thousands of dollars. President Kennedy's golf clubs were sold for $772,500 (858 times Sotheby's estimate); $453,500 was paid for his rocking-chair, which Sotheby's estimated would be sold for $3,000–5,000.

Fans covet autographs and signed photographs of celebrities, preferably delivered with a 'personal' message to the fan. The Hard Rock Café chain displays rock memorabilia and rotates them between branches. Celebrity artefacts like automobiles, clothes, shoes, beds and guitars are prized. Indeed, celebrity homes are often preserved as shrines, or when they are put on the open market, value is added to the price because of the association with celebrity. Visits to Graceland, Elvis Presley's Tennessee home, are regarded by fans as analogous to the Christian pilgrimage. The number of visitors per annum is remarkable: 750,000, a figure that comfortably eclipses the visitor total for The White House. The homes of George Washington, Thomas Jefferson, Abraham Lincoln and Eva Peron have similar iconic status. If only cranks see Elvis as a holy figure, the belief in his capacity for reincarnation is amazingly widespread among his fans. Elvis died in 1977, yet sightings of him occur regularly. An entire sub-genre of celebrity literature is devoted to the proposition that his death was merely a staged event.

Cemeteries that contain the remains of celebrities are also popular tourist attractions, just as cathedrals housing the graves of saints were once popular places of pilgrimage. Père Lachaise in Paris, Highgate in London, the Hollywood and Westwood cemeteries in Los Angeles, are among the most popular destinations. Highgate now even charges an entry fee. Paying to visit the graves of George Eliot, Ralph Richardson and Karl Marx in Highgate cemetery may prove that death provides no obstacle to the commodification of the celebrity. But it is eclipsed by the product innovation now available at the Hollywood Memorial Cemetery in Los Angeles. Colloquially known as the Valhalla of Hollywood, it is the final resting place of Rudolph Valentino, Tyrone Power, Cecil B. DeMille, Douglas Fairbanks, Nelson Eddy, Bugsy Siegel, Peter Lorre, John Huston, Mel Blanc, Peter Finch and several other stellar Hollywood *habitués*. Facing bankruptcy at the end of the 1990s, the site was taken over, rebranded as 'Forever Hollywood', and marketed as the Valhalla of the stars. Budget internment in the 60-acre site currently costs $637, which includes a specially made video of the deceased that is replayed on a big screen during the ceremony, incorporating highlights from home videos. For executive interment, in the vicinity of a Hollywood star grave, prices currently fetch as much as $5,000. The move has transformed the finances of Forever Hollywood. The number of funerals has increased twenty-fold since the marketing campaign began.

Forever Hollywood offers the fan the ultimate *kitsch* experience – becoming a posthumous neighbour of the celebrity in afterlife. The desire to be joined to a celebrity, even in death, further underlines the peculiar seduction of celebrity culture. At the death of a celebrity, it is quite common for fans to carry away flowers and message tags from wreaths and even handfuls of burial earth as relics. The headstones of James Dean, Dylan Thomas, Sylvia Plath, Buddy Holly and Jim Morrison have all been stolen.

Even grave-robbing plays a part in celebrity culture. In 1876 the shimmering cultic significance of Abraham Lincoln for the American nation resulted in a bizarre attempt to steal his body from its resting place in the Oak Ridge Cemetery at Springfield, Illinois. A gang hatched a conspiracy to use the body as ransom to persuade the state of Illinois to release an imprisoned criminal. The plan was foiled. However, fears that the grave-robbers might strike again persuaded the authorities to remove the casket from the sarcophagus and secrete it in a place of greater safety. For eleven years tourists who came to pay their respects at Lincoln's grave gazed at what was actually an empty tomb, thus perhaps unwittingly illustrating a central insight into the true nature of celebrity, namely that façade is crucial. In 1886 Lincoln's body was re-interred in a new grave. However, when its monument was found to be settling unevenly, the casket was again shifted. Robert Lincoln, the President's son, determined that state officials and grave-robbers would never cause his father's body to be moved again. He had seen a new device, used in the burial of the Chicago tycoon George M. Pullman, a steel cage erected around the coffin and filled with cement. In 1901 Lincoln was reburied, this time in a canopy of cement and steel.

Strangely, the bizarre movements of Lincoln's corpse are not without comparison in celebrity culture. In 1978 the body of Charlie Chaplin was snatched from Vevey cemetery in Switzerland and, in an unusual case of celebrity 'posthumous kidnapping', a ransom of 600,000 Swiss francs was demanded. The police eventually captured the conspirators and recovered the body.

In Christian religion, bread and wine symbolize Christ's body. Consuming them in communion symbolizes the sharing of Christ's body in this world, and is honoured as confirmation in the reality of the supreme creator. In celebrity culture the scattering of ashes is a similar, albeit secularized, rite of sharing. The scattering of Bill Shankly's ashes on the turf of Anfield, home of Liverpool Football Club, symbolized both Shankly's god-like status among fans and a sense of continuity with the values and success associated with his management. Scattering the ashes of sports celebrities around a stadium with which they have strong associations is now relatively common.

Interestingly, celebrity bears no moral connection with moral elevation. Notoriety is an equivalent source of public fascination. For example, members of the families of Jeffrey Dahmer's victims planned to auction the serial killer's instruments of torture and divide the proceeds. Although their plan was thwarted, public interest in owning the artefacts was considerable. In Britain, similar controversy was aroused by plans to sell 25 Cromwell Street, Gloucester. This was the so-called 'house of horror' in which the serial killers Fred and Rosemary West tortured and murdered their victims. The controversy turned on commercial interests that aspired to memorialize the site as a 'museum' to caution the public against the infernal wiles of transgression. The local council eventually decided to demolish the house. Disposal arrangements for the bricks, timber and mortar were shrouded in secrecy so as to deter ghoulish souvenir hunters.

The St Thomas Effect

The expression 'doubting Thomas' derives from the biblical story of St Thomas. When Christ appeared to the Apostles after the Resurrection, it was Thomas who vehemently doubted his presence until he touched the wounds of crucifixion on Christ's body. The term *St Thomas effect* refers to the compulsion to authenticate a desired object by travelling to it, touching it and photographing it. Fans manifest the St Thomas effect in stalking and mobbing celebrities and in obsessively constructing celebrity reliquaries. The imaginary relation of intimacy with the celebrity translates into the overwhelming wish to touch the celebrity, or possess celebrity heirlooms or other discarded items. The intensity of desire aroused in the St Thomas effect may result in the suspension of self-control, which can place both fan and celebrity at personal risk.

For example, in July 2000, Karen Burke, a 19-year-old student, was put on probation for harassing the feminist writer and celebrity Germaine Greer. The court was told that Burke was infatuated with Dr Greer, and wanted to adopt her as a 'spiritual mother figure'. She engaged in peripatetic correspondence with Greer, which terminated when Greer decided that Burke was possibly in need of psychiatric help. Burke developed intense feelings of dependency and travelled to Greer's house, where she was graciously accommodated in the summerhouse. The next day Greer drove Burke to Cambridge to catch a train. Within 48 hours Burke returned to the house, and Greer rang the police to have her removed. The following day Burke returned again. When Greer became alarmed and threatened to call the police, Burke pinioned her, crying 'Mummy, Mummy don't do that!' For about two hours a struggle ensued, in the course of which both Greer and Burke were hurt. The incident ended when friends – whom the writer had arranged to meet – arrived at the house and found Burke screaming and clinging to Greer's legs. The incident must have been extremely distressing for both parties. But it illustrates how the imaginary relation that a fan has with a celebrity can sometimes escalate, from the wish to authenticate the desired object, to an overpowering determination to establish the truth of their presence, to authenticate them by grabbing them or holding on to them.

The passionate concern of many fans to authenticate celebrity arte-facts is perhaps in direct proportion to the abstract desire that the fan nurtures to possess the celebrity. Celebrities are elusive and inaccessible. In contrast, celebrity artefacts can be possessed and cherished. However, the artefact is only worth having if its relationship to the celebrity can be veri-fied. If a relationship with the personification of abstract desire cannot be consummated, the inanimate artefact at least enables the fan to savour proximate possession of the celebrity.

Celebrity and Death

The pilgrims who flock to Graceland, the burial place and former home of Elvis Presley, do not so much honour a dead God as proclaim the presence of a living secular one in popular culture. Many fans believe that Elvis faked his death so as to retire from the intrusions of celebrity culture. Even those who accept his death as a literal fact regard him as a living cultural presence.

Conversely, the death of John Lennon is not disputed, either by fans or the mass-media. Even so, he remains a superhuman, inspirational figure for millions. Lennon was certainly conscious of the extraordinary power of celebrity in popular culture. His comment in the 1960s – that The Beatles were more popular than Jesus Christ – drew outrage in the press and led to public burnings of Beatles records by some religious groups in America. However, it was arguably true. Like religion, Beatles music in the 1960s seemed to communicate the incommunicable.

Lennon clearly found it difficult to cope with fame. His lyric in *The Ballad of John & Yoko* – that 'the way things are going they're gonna crucify me' – suggests he was suffering from a Christ complex. Certainly, the ill-thought-out interventions into politics during the 1970s suggested that he was consciously trying to save the world. Was not Lennon's journey from working-class Liverpool to celestial stardom in the 1960s and '70s a parallel of Christ's journey from the wayside inn's manger to become the 'light of the world'? And did not Lennon's assassination in 1980, at the hands of a deranged fan, echo Christ's death on the cross? For some people, the spiritual comparisons are unmistakable. Against this, if Lennon sometimes presented himself as a messiah-like figure, his sense of the absurdity of celebrity and his irreverence nearly always deflated this public 'face'. While Lennon's ability to engender collective effervescence in audiences is legendary, his worldliness was never an issue. Figuratively speaking, Lennon may have transported audiences to sky and underworld, but he was emphatically of the earth.

Stalkers

The long police hunt to find the killer of the BBC TV presenter Jill Dando, murdered in 1999, uncovered 180 men who harboured unnatural fixations on her. The police pursued two theories in their line of enquiry. First, that Dando's role as a presenter of the popular TV show *Crimewatch*, inspired a contract killing from a professional hitman. Second, that she was a victim of a crazed stalker. When a reward for information failed to generate information from the Underworld, the police concluded that they were probably looking for a lone stalker.

The psychological profile that the police constructed suggested that the man they were seeking was either divorced or lived alone. They suspected that he tried to contact Dando by letter, fax, phone or email but either failed to reach her, or was rebuffed. They found evidence of attempts to get details of her electricity, gas, water and telephone bills. If this was the work of one man, the police speculated, it was reasonable to assume that, driven by frustration, anger or jealousy, he began to plot his revenge.

As Dando's wedding approached, his obsession with her increased. A glamorous photograph of her on the cover of the *Radio Times* may have sparked his decision to kill her. Witness accounts suggest that he travelled to her house and probably loitered around the premises on three or four occasions on different days before shooting her in the back of the head on her doorstep. The psychological profile eventually resulted in the police arresting and charging a local man, Barry George, with the murder in May 2000. He was convicted at the Old Bailey in July 2001.

The notion that para-social interaction is fundamental in engendering and reproducing celebrity culture is well established. Celebrities are often said to exert a magnetic attraction over fans. However, this magnetism typically operates through the organized mobilization of fantasy and desire. Essential to the concept of para-social interaction is that the relationship is at bottom imaginary. The overwhelming majority of celebrities and fans do not actually know one another or engage in face-to-face interaction. In addition, celebrities maintain a distinction between the celebrity public face and the veridical self. But occasionally, the magnetic attraction of the public face erodes the distinction. In such cases celebrities may experience the mortification of the veridical self and fans may foster obses-sional-compulsive neurosis.

This type of neurosis may perpetuate fantasies of seducing or possess-ing celebrities. The fan who suffers from obsessional-compulsive neurosis is incapable of mentally recognizing the staged reciprocity between celebri-ties and audiences in public settings, and instead imagines that this reciprocity is validated in the relationship between the celebrity and the fan. It matters not that the relationship is basically imaginary, because its effects in organizing the emotions and lifestyle of the fan are real.

Symptoms of obsessional-compulsive neurosis in fans include devour-ing news data on celebrities, creating scrapbooks and files, finding out the addresses of celebrity homes from the internet, loitering near such premises, generating unsolicited and unwelcome letters, telephone calls, electronic mail, graffiti, and, in some cases, engaging in physical and sexual assaults. From the standpoint of the fan, the organization of his or her habitual life course around the imagined routines and public responsibili-ties of the celebrity, merely confirms the reality of the reciprocity between the fan and the celebrity. However, this reciprocity is founded on abstract desire and depends on imaginary relations appearing to be tenable.

Stalking is one of the most extreme manifestations of this behaviour. Indeed stalking may be defined as the development of an obsessional-compulsive neurosis in respect of a celebrity, which results in intrusive shadowing and/or harassment. It is often associated with abandonment, rejection and feelings of low self-esteem. Interestingly, stalking is not confined to celebrity culture. The UK Parliament passed the Protection from Harassment Act in 1997 so as to protect the privacy of individuals from non-reciprocated, intrusive interest from others. In 1998, no less than 2,221 people were convicted of stalking under the terms of the Act. By 1994, 48 US states had passed anti-stalking legislation, and nearly 200,000 reports were investigated. Ordinary people experience harass-ment from stalkers. But the high public profile of celebrities, and the peculiar imaginary nature of para-social desire and recognition, make celebrities the stalkers' prime target.

The mass-media has awarded a high profile to cases of celebrity stalking in recent years. Famous cases include Monica Seles, stabbed by Gunther Parche, who had a long history of obsession with Steffi Graf. Madonna, who was stalked for five years by Robert Dewey Hoskins, who threatened to 'slice her from ear to ear'. Helena Bonham-Carter, who was stalked for six years by Andrew Farquharson. Michael J. Fox, who received 5,000 letters, usually filled with rabbit droppings, from one fan. Klaus Wagner, who trailed Princess Diana to protect her from a 'Satan conspiracy' supposedly conducted against her by the Queen. Brooke Shields who was stalked by Ronald Bailey for fifteen years, which resulted in a court order in September 2000 to keep away from her for at least a decade, or go to prison. Ulrika Jonsson, who was bombarded with obscene phone calls and nude photos by Peter Casey, who threw himself under a train after police questioning. And Lady Helen Taylor, who was stalked by Simon Reynolds, who eventually killed himself.

The search for fame is often an unambiguous motive in stalking. Mick Abram, who stabbed former Beatle George Harrison on 30 December 1999, boasted on Christmas Eve to his ex-partner that 'I am going to be famous'. Abram, a former heroin addict, was reported to suffer from a deep-seated paranoid psychosis that turned into an obsession with The Beatles, and particularly Harrison, whom Abram believed was a witch.

Stalking brutally underlines the power of celebrity to arouse deep, irrational emotions. In the psychology of the stalker, unconsummated desire is distorted into an overpowering wish to achieve consummation or recognition. This wish may be irrational, but it is generally premeditated and establishes itself as the ultimate end of conduct. Stalkers regard celebrities as magical figures or demons, and stalking as a way of communing with magic. By executing the celebrity, the stalker either validates his or her superior power or eliminates from the world the magic that has turned into a cause of irritation and distress. Abram's purpose in seeking to murder Harrison was to save the world from what he took to be a demonic force.

Shamanism in Rock and Film Culture

The connection between shamanism and popular music goes back to the birth of the Blues, which, in the Southern states of the USA was known as 'the Devil's music'. The murder of the Delta blues-man Robert Johnson in 1938, poisoned by drinking strychnine from an unsealed bottle of whisky, created a shamanic hero of the Blues, virtually overnight. In the 1940s and '50s the stereotype was taken over by jazz musicians like Charlie Parker, Miles Davis and John Coltrane, whose playing and transgressive lifestyles were yoked, in the public imagination, by supernatural powers. Coltrane must be the only celebrity to have a church founded in his name: St John's African Orthodox Church in San Francisco. In their best work Coltrane and Davis achieved a purity of expression that was indeed religious in its intensity. Yet precisely because it carried the capacity to transport audiences away from earthly cares, it was associated with possession and magic, thus reinforcing the links with shamanism and the devil.

But, arguably, it was not until the emergence of rock in the 1960s that the twinning of the shaman with certain types of charismatic musical personality became uniform. Jimi Hendrix, Jim Morrison, Mick Jagger, Lou Reed, Iggy Pop, Marc Bolan and David Bowie consciously presented themselves as shamanic figures. Bowie invented the part of the alien rock messiah 'Ziggy Stardust'. As with Pete Townshend's earlier creation of the eponymous youth messiah in *Tommy* (1968), it was never exactly clear what Ziggy Stardust's sacred mission involved, or who he was interested in saving. The content of religious convictions did not matter. Rather it was the state of collective effervescence that these characters induced that was the main lever of their cultural power.

Shamanism is a potent source of fantasy and self-delusion. Alan Parker's film *The Wall* (1982) emphasized the thin line between rock shamanism and Fascism. The concentration on image, might and moral certainty occurs in both genres. In 1976 David Bowie outraged the media and many of his fans by apparently greeting them with a Nazi salute when he arrived at Victoria railway station from the Continent. The press publicised his comment made to a Swedish reporter that 'Britain could benefit from a Fascist leader'. Not surprisingly, Bowie later recanted, and explained his flirtation with Nazism as a by-product of physical and psychological exhaustion. However, the mythologizing aspects of Nazism, notably the passionate concern with regeneration and the search for new order, has strong overtones with the myths of finding spiritual wholeness and emotional integration through worshipping the *Übermensch*, the prototypal celebrity in Nietzsche's philosphy.

However, in this regard, the fate of the hated statue of Stalin that stood at Letna Plain overlooking the Vltava river in Prague is perhaps instructive. Unveiled at the peak of Communist power in 1955, the 14,000-ton, 98-feet-high granite statue was the largest figure of Stalin ever erected. Khruschev denounced Stalin in the following year, leaving the Czech Communist Party with a prominent and embarrassing white elephant. The monument was eventually blown up in 1962, but the plinth remained as a reminder to the Czech public of *temps perdu*. In 1996 it was occupied by a ten-metre-high inflatable replica of Michael Jackson, who was passing through the city on his latest world tour, which, one may ruefully note, was called 'History'.

The rock shaman produces excitement and mass hysteria rather than religious salvation. The ability to act as a conducting rod of mass desire, and to precipitate semi-orgiastic emotions in the crowd, are the most obvious features of this form of shamanic power. When an attempt is made to articulate or codify creeds, it usually falls flat. Coltrane boiled down his religious conviction into two words: 'live right'. The message of

The Beatles was equally attractive yet just as tenuous: 'All you need is love'. The efforts by later rock shamans, such as Michael Jackson, Marvin Gaye, Kurt Cobain, Michael Hutchence, Bono and Liam Gallagher, to express a creed of living, are confused and often embarrassing. 'All you need is love' is a truism, but one that obviously glosses over many difficulties and inconsistencies.

Perhaps one reason for the significance attributed to these simplistic celebrity philosophies is that they are generally presented to an audience that is peculiarly impressionable. Typically, rock shamans address youth cultures. For people who are consciously seeking role models that contrast with the models of family life, passionate convictions, delivered with sincerity and glamour, have a strong resonance. In societies where rates of divorce are high, and where the future of the nuclear family is in doubt, celebrities are notable 'significant others' in the public management of emotions. Because youths are the immediate 'victims' of divorce and marital troubles, the impact of celebrity culture is likely to be particularly strong on them.

However, it is a mistake to limit this impact to the status of youth. Judy Garland's iconic status in gay culture partly derived from her ability to cope with disapproval, rejection and marginalization. The enduring celebrity of Marilyn Monroe derives from her projection of vulnerability as a mode of communication with her audience. Monroe enables audiences of all ages to escape the category of their private worries and troubles by identifying with her highly public personal difficulties.

Yet it is undoubtedly in youth culture that the category of celebrity possesses deepest force. This is one reason why the method of rock celebrity presentation is usually intensely sexual. As cultural icons they adopt the public face of a sexual object. Because their mass appeal depends on presenting themselves as constantly available, their stage dress and presentation coaxes crowds to want them, especially in the sexual sense. The fantasies born as youths listen to a CD or tape in their parents' home or in a bedsit are part of the energy used in the stage performance, which presents the performer as someone who apparently lives without taboos. 'Jesus died for somebody else's sins, but not mine', declared Patti Smith in the 1975 album *Horses*.

The absence of guilt and taboos are also prominent motifs in Hollywood celebrity culture. The shaman figure in Hollywood is typically associated with amoral and dangerous influence. Rudolph Valentino in the Jazz Age symbolized the threat that male American audiences professed in the face of 'erotic outsiders'. For females, Valentino was an object of desire precisely because his body and behaviour refused to comply with ethnocentric masculine stereotypes. For males, he was condemned as an indolent foreigner whose public face concealed the genetic inferiority attributed to all such immigrants.

Moral panics about the amoral attitude of Hollywood on sexual questions in the 1920s were replaced in the 1930s with fears about the influence of violence in gangster films. Movies like *Doorway to Hell* and *Little Caesar* (both 1930), *Scarface* (1931) and *Public Enemy* (1932) were criticized for glorifying violence. Actors associated with gangster roles, such as Edward G. Robinson, Paul Muni, George Raft and James Cagney, were vilified for playing parts that taught audiences that crime does pay. The gangster movies seemed to comment directly on the perceived American lust for money, and the invalidation of American males in repressing their desires. Robinson's mobster, Rico Bandello in *Little Caesar*, is evidently a psychopath, but the film is ambiguous about others who, unlike Rico, simply accept their lot as jobsworths and stable family men. They will never have Rico's wealth, or experience his unbridled aggression. They must rein in and disguise their desires and thus, the film suggests, they cannot, like Rico, ultimately be true to themselves.

In the 1950s, Elvis Presley, James Dean and Marlon Brando symbolized the lust for money and violated stereotypes of masculine invalidation in other ways. They were obviously profligate with money; they prioritized self-expression over conformity, and they placed hedonism above responsibility. In the eyes of the moral majority, unlike Valentino who symbolized 'foreignness', they were 'the enemy within' – the youthful, ingrate inheritors of the sacrifices made by the adults of Eisenhower's generation who had defeated Hitler and Tojo in the Second World War. Their *insouciance* was an affront to the work ethic that demanded relentless endeavour in the workplace and sobriety at home.

David Riesman captured the state of public anxiety that existed in the early 1950s with his famous distinction between 'inner' and 'other' directed personalities.[7] Inner-directed personalities are the archetype of pioneering stock, who rely on the Bible, the example of their parents and their own efforts and energies to construct a tenable moral framework and make their way in the world. Other-directed types abandon internalized moral systems in favour of the fashions and fads of the mass-media. It was the seductive role model that Presley, Dean and Brando presented to impressionable, other-directed types that so perplexed the moral majority in the 1950s. Riesman was troubled with the fear that Western society had already exchanged the principle that work is the central life interest for an addiction to consumption as the end of life. Further, the Hollywood stars expressed this metamorphosis in highly conspicuous and morally dangerous ways.

The exiled Frankfurt School theorist Leo Lowenthal had already anticipated an historical dimension to this thesis. He argued that, in the 1920s and '30s, American popular culture exchanged its respect for figures of industry and administration, such as Thomas Edison and Teddy Roosevelt, for the adulation of show business idols, such as Charlie Chaplin, James Cagney, Al Jolson, Clara Bow, Theda Bara and Mae West. For Lowenthal, the entertainment celebrity was now the most desired object in popular culture, leaving the traditional role models of industrial society – the inventor, the teacher and the public official – stranded.

For the moral majority in 1950s America, Hollywood celebrity was a deeply ambivalent construct. The wealth, freedom and popularity of stars fulfilled the American dream. Hollywood celebrities were self-made individuals who achieved their wealth and power by their talents and industry. This was in stark contrast with the inherited wealth of the lazy, self-approving European aristocracy or the children of the American *nouveaux riches* that the economist Thorstein Veblen had rebuked in his attack on the perils of conspicuous consumption. Conversely, Hollywood celebrity was also regarded as the worm in the bud of the American dream. Stars worked, but unlike other Americans, they seemed to enjoy their work. They were paid, but by the standards of Middle America, they received a king's ransom for their labour. Moreover, in the highly public reporting of the sex lives of Hollywood celebrities, Middle America sat goggle-eyed at the freedom from moral restraint and public censure enjoyed by the celebritariat.

Hollywood film directors have exploited the popular association between celebrity and superhuman powers. Oliver Stone's film *The Doors* (1991) was built on the premise that, as a child, Jim Morrison's spirit was possessed by the spirit of an Amer-Indian shaman. For Stone, nothing but *mana* could explain Morrison's uncanny ability to encourage audiences to shed inhibitions and be carried outside themselves.

Inviting Hollywood celebrities to play the role of the Devil and take the audience on a journey into the Underworld is also a theme in American film. In recent years, Robert De Niro (*Angel Heart*, 1986), Jack Nicholson (*The Witches of Eastwick*, 1987) and Al Pacino (*The Devil's Advocate*, 1997) have played the Devil, while Brad Pitt has played Death (*Meet Joe Black*, 1999). The choice of these actors is revealing. Each of them has claim to be regarded as a shamanic emblem for their generation. In a variety of films in the 1970s and '80s, De Niro and Pacino played rebels, anti-heroes, outsiders and romantic misfits who symbolized the rebellious and misplaced sense of identity in large sections of the audience. Jack Nicholson broke through to mainstream audiences with *Easy Rider* (1969), a *succès de scandale* in Hollywood, not only for its controversial content but for its enormous box-office appeal too, which briefly created independent film-making as a sunrise industry. Brad Pitt in *Fight Club* (1998) played the ultimate shamanic figure by representing the id (Dionysus) to Edward Norton's ego (Apollo).

Celebrity Ceremonies of Ascent

Celebrity culture is secular. Because the roots of secular society lie in Christianity, many of the symbols of success and failure in celebrity draw on myths and rites of religious ascent and descent.

Celebrity culture is not organized around a system of ecumenical values that link this-worldly conduct to salvation. Nor should one underestimate the complexity of modalities of celebrity culture, each with its specific beliefs, myths, rites and symbols. The variety and diversity of celebrity culture is a constant barrier to meaningful generalization. Yet, without wishing to minimize these analytical problems, honour and notoriety are, very often, prominent features of the celebrity status economy, and money is typically the currency in which honour and notoriety are measured.

The rise of celebrity culture is, indeed, intimately connected with the rise of a money economy and the growth of populations concentrated in urban–industrial locations. It is partly a product of the world of the stranger, wherein the individual is uprooted from family and community and relocated in the anonymous city, in which social relations are often glancing, episodic and unstable. Just as the Puritan in the seventeenth century looked to Christ for comfort and inspiration, fans today, like Joanne mentioned at the beginning of this chapter, seek out celebrities to anchor or support personal life. The dominant motive here is not salva-tion. Fans are attracted to celebrities for a variety of reasons, with sexual attraction, admiration of unique personal values and mass-media acclaim being prominent. Hardly any believe that celebrities can 'save' them in an orthodox religious or quasi-religious sense. But most find comfort, glamour or excitement in attaching themselves to a celebrity. Through this attachment a sense of glamorous difference is enunciated.

In a money economy the shaman's belief in the supreme being above and the underworld below is diminished, as is the Christian belief in God and the Devil. Yet if the religious division between earth, sky and underworld is mitigated, consciousness of material success and failure is accentuated. Celebrity culture has developed a variety of ceremonies of ascent and descent to symbolize honorific status and the loss of it. The central ascension beliefs and rites are organized around three themes: elevation, magic and immortality.

Elevation refers to the social and cultural processes involved in raising the celebrity above the public. Elevation is literally achieved in Hollywood celebrity because the magnified screen and billboard images are raised above the eye-level of cinema-goers. The wealth and luxury of celebrities are staple, and instantly recognized, symbols of success in market society.

Further evidence of elevation is found in the ubiquity of celebrity biographies in popular culture. Popular, mass-circulation magazines like *Hello* and *OK* are largely devoted to glossy photo-journalism, documenting the marriages, houses, holidays, divorces, births, medical operations, and deaths of celebrities. The TV talk show, such as *Parkinson*, *Larry King Live*, *The Late Show with David Letterman* and the *Jay Leno Show*, enhances the image of celebrities as figures of significance by affording them the opportunity to present a variation on the public face in, so to speak, 'out of role' contexts.

The TV talk show was invented in America in 1950, when Jerry Lester started hosting a five-nights-a-week show called *Broadway Open House*. However, the form was defined by Johnny Carson, a former stand-up comedian turned host. Carson first presented *The Tonight Show* in 1962. Most commentators agree that he dominated the medium until his retirement in 1993. Carson cultivated the talk show as a vehicle for celebrity indiscretion and revelation. His invention of the role of the talk-show host was a continuation of the close-up technique, by purporting to offer audiences more intimate, out-of-face encounters, with celebrities. (D. W. Griffith, who directed the first full-length feature film, *Birth of a Nation*, in 1915 is generally regarded to have invented the close-up shot, which enabled audiences to see not only the faces of stars but the portrayal of emotions too, thus intensifying the intimacy between the audience and the star.) The set design of *The Tonight Show* conveyed the impression that the studio was an extension of Carson's own home. By identifying the set with domesticity, *The Tonight Show* established the chat show as a relaxed and friendly after dinner tête-à-tête rather than a public confrontation. Later generations of talk shows copied the format by using carpets, rugs, flowers in vases, sofas, easy chairs and *trompe l'œil* background windows to convey a sense of reassuring domesticity.

Elevation is a perpetual feature of the honorific status of celebrity. Generally, it is geared to market requirements. Thus, when Tom Cruise, Tom Hanks, Britney Spears, Janet Jackson, John Grisham or Will Self has a new film, album or book to plug, they become the subject of a media saturation campaign by the companies selling the product. A common technique in marketing campaigns is to require the celebrity to participate in out-of-face encounters with chat-show hosts. Plugging a product on TV is more effective if celebrities use the occasion to open up, and reveal personality layers that are hidden from the screen persona. However, celebrity interviews are only effective if the essential role distance between the celebrity and the audience is maintained. Celebrities may slip out of role in chat show interviews so as to appear more human. But if they do so continuously they neutralize the charisma on which their status as exalted and extraordinary figures depends.

Celebrity power depends on immediate public recognition. As we shall see, celebrities often feel hunted by the devouring public. The silent film star Clara Bow complained, 'When they stare at me, I get the creeps.'

Harrison Ford attested that 'I'm very uncomfortable when people stare at me.'[8] Without wishing to minimize the sincerity of these sentiments, we should place them in the context of celebrity motivation. Instant public acclaim is part of the appeal of being a celebrity. Along with the wealth and the flexible lifestyle, it is one of the reasons why achieved celebrity is sought after with such deliberate and often frenzied ardour.

Magic, the second theme, is invoked by the shaman, who partly asserts and reinforces his power through the performance of various tricks and undertakings. Celebrities cultivate the same practice. Hollywood celebrities are able to perform magical feats on celluloid. Action-movie stars like John Wayne, Robert Mitchum, Harrison Ford, Bruce Willis, Mel Gibson and Pierce Brosnan are frequently required to perform remarkable and magical feats on screen. Sports celebrities like David Beckham, Romario, Ronaldo, Wayne Gretsky, Brian Lara, Kapil Dev, Mark McGwire, Conchita Martinez, Venus Williams, Tiger Woods and Anna Kournikova are expected to do the same thing in the sports arena.

Edgar Morin contends that there is a spillover effect between the role incarnated by an actor in a performance and the public perception of the actor. 'From their union', he writes, 'is born a composite creature who participates in both, envelops them both: the star'.[9] It is this spillover effect that contributes to the public perception of the celebrity as a magical, cultural colossus. Part of the appeal of the Planet Hollywood restaurant chain is the idea that diners have access to major celebrity investors, notably Bruce Willis, Demi Moore, Sylvester Stallone and Arnold Schwarzenegger. The restaurants display celebrity artefacts, and the celebrities make scheduled live appearances. Planet Hollywood memorabilia and star appearances are calculated with mathematical precision to give the illusion of proximity to celebrity. Yet face-to-face encounters are so rare as to belong to the realm of exotica. Bodyguards, publicists and 'impression managers' constitute key elements in the celebrity retinue that manage the presentation of the celebrity face to the public. Public appearances of celebrities are not always accompanied with a roll of drums, although, interestingly, heavy drumbeats are often used in shamanic rites to summon spirits. However, public appearances of celebrities are generally staged events in which publicists, bodyguards and public relations staff announce and manage contact between the celebrity and fans. The celebrity retinue enhances the aura of magic that surrounds the celebrity. Their pomp and mass announces to the public that a figure of significance has descended to – so to speak – break bread with them.

As for *immortality*, the third theme, in secular society the honorific status conferred on certain celebrities outlasts physical death. Madame Tussaud imported her wax museum from France into England in 1802. It consisted of a collection of celebrity manikins. It was of huge interest to audiences that had never seen photographs of the great celebrities and notorious criminals of the day. It supplemented the engravings of famous personages widely coveted in the eighteenth century. Celebrity immortality is obviously more readily achieved in the era of mass communications, since film footage and sound recordings preserve the celebrity in the public sphere. Mass communication preserves the cultural capital of celebrities and increases their chances of becoming immortal in the public sphere. Graham McCann, pondering the immortality of Marilyn Monroe, notes the central paradox of celebrity immortality: 'Monroe is now everywhere yet nowhere: her image is on walls, in movies, in books – all after-images, obscuring the fact of her permanent absence.'[10]

Descent and Falling

Celebrities take themselves and their fans higher. They are the ambassadors of the celestial sphere. But they can also descend to the underworld, and drag their fans down with them. Hitler is arguably the twentieth century's principal example of celebrity ascent and descent. His astonishing rise to power was, at first, internationally acclaimed as an example of a strong leader presiding over the rebirth of a nation. Millions of Germans developed passionate, deep, not to say irrational feelings of devotion towards him and genuinely regarded him to be their real Führer, i.e., their 'leader'. However, as the true extent of his intrigue, callousness and brutality became exposed, he was turned into a global pariah. Some even regarded him as the incarnation of the Anti-Christ. As the vanity of his military ambitions was revealed, by crushing defeats on the Russian Front, by the persistence of the British and the Resistance movements on the Continent, and by America's entry into the war, he literally became unhinged. Before his suicide in the command bunker in Berlin he raved against the German people for their cowardice and issued instructions for a scorched-earth policy to spoil the fruits of victory for the Allies. The unutterable disgrace of his genocidal practices became a millennial standard of inhumanity, which post-Nazi Germany has failed to erase entirely.

Descent and falling are twinned with ascent and rising. Elevation is, in itself, a source of envy as well as approval. Celebrities acquire so much honorific status and wealth that their downfall becomes a matter of public speculation and, on occasion, is even desired. Sometimes this provokes conspiracy. Orson Welles based a female character in *Citizen Kane* (1941) on the mistress of the media tycoon William Randolph Hearst. Indeed, the demonic figure of Kane himself is widely believed to be based on Hearst. The tycoon's revenge was to conduct an unstinting campaign against Welles and the film in the mass-media. Welles even alleged that Hearst planted an under-age girl in his hotel bedroom. A scandal was only averted by a tip-off to Welles from the police. Hearst certainly damaged Welles's reputation, and contributed to his later difficulties in gaining finance to develop his film work. Similarly, public disquiet about Charlie Chaplin's private life and media reports of his apparent sympathy with Communism resulted in him being barred from McCarthyite America. The mass-media who build up celebrities are often unable to resist engineering their downfall.

Celebrities, however, also collude in bringing about their own descent. The inventories of alcoholism, drug addiction, mania and depression constructed by Kenneth Anger, Gary Herman and Dave Thompson of celebrities in film and rock support the commonsense intuition that constantly being in the public eye produces psychological difficulties and trauma. The public face estranges the veridical self and results in fears of personal disappearance or annihilation. Public appearances become associated with self-denial, or confirm, in the sight of the celebrity, that the veridical self has been destroyed. The public face becomes a living tomb of staged personality. Addictive, maniacal and obsessive behaviour are the corollaries of chronic feelings of helplessness and inauthenticity. Celebrities often feel both personally unworthy after receiving public adulation and out of control of their own careers. Celebrities suffer an abnormally high incidence of mania, schizophrenia, paranoia and psychopathic behaviour.

Descent is established by routines of behaviour that centre on the mortification of the body. Thus, celebrities may become anorexic or balloon in weight, develop phobias about being in public places, succumb to narcotic addiction or engage in public displays of drunkenness. The mortification of the body brings the celebrity down to earth. In cases of suicide and attempted suicide, it literally seeks to bury the body under the earth. Outwardly, suicide is a destructive act, but inwardly it offers the celebrity permanent refuge from a rapacious public.

The theme of mortification in the rites surrounding celebrity descent seems to take three general forms: scourging, disintegration and redemption. *Scourging* refers to a process of status-stripping in which the honorific status of the celebrity is systematically degraded. It has two forms: *auto-degradation*, in which the primary exponent of status-stripping is the celebrity, and *exo-degradation*, in which external parties, usually situated in the mass-media, are the architects of the status-stripping process. In general the ceremonies surrounding both forms interrelate and are mutually reinforcing.

The celebrated 1960s soccer star George Best was arguably the greatest player of his generation. However, the media and fan expectations of producing a world-class performance every week resulted in gambling and drink problems. After Manchester United won the European Cup in 1968, Best felt strongly that aging players in the team should be replaced. When the manager, Matt Busby, proved reluctant to buy new stars, Best became disenchanted. This reinforced his alcohol dependence and alienated him from other members of the team, and eventually from the manager too. Best became prone to temper tantrums and unpredictable behaviour. Gradually, he became a liability to the team and in his late twenties decided to retire from soccer. Best blamed himself for not being able to withstand the pressures of soccer stardom, but he was also condemned by the media for squandering his gifts.

The snooker player Alex 'Hurricane' Higgins was the victim of similar pressures. He dealt with the strain of trying to please his fans with magical skills every time he played by developing a dependence on alcohol. His playing became increasingly erratic and his public outbursts were frequently savage.

James Fox, the star of *The Servant* (1963), *The Chase* (1966) and *Performance* (1970), is another example of a celebrity who became prey to addictive, self-destructive behaviour. He despaired of the superficial values of Hollywood and became oppressed by what he saw as the inadequacy of his public face. Fox abandoned acting for ten years. He joined a religious sect and became involved in community work. It was not until the early 1980s that he returned to the screen.

Lena Zavaroni, the British child star, died from anorexia in adulthood. Margaux Hemingway and Princess Diana suffered from bulimia. Media speculation about apparent dramatic weight loss has surrounded Calista Flockhart and Portia de Rossi of *Ally McBeal*, Jennifer Aniston of *Friends* and Victoria Beckham of The Spice Girls. Richey Edwards of the Manic Street Preachers engaged in self-mutilation, suffered from depression and alcohol problems, and in 1995 abruptly vanished and is presumed dead. Sid Vicious and Kurt Cobain displayed erratic drug-related behaviour, seemed unable to cope with fame, and both committed suicide, one by a heroin overdose, the other by means of a bullet to the head. Elizabeth Taylor, Elvis Presley, Marlon Brando, Roseanne Barr, Elton John and Oprah Winfrey fought highly public battles with their weight.

Examples of celebrity auto- and exo-degradation could be endlessly added. The point that needs to be re-emphasized here is that status-stripping ceremonies are typically focused on the body. The mortification of idealized masculine and feminine celebrity constructions centres on the scourging of the body, which includes ripping, cutting, shedding, flailing and, conversely, overeating, addiction, agoraphobia and claustrophobia.

In extreme cases, scourging results in a status-stripping vortex – *disintegration* – that leads the celebrity to conclude that nothing can be salvaged, because nothing remains in the veridical self which is recognized as trustworthy or worth saving. The resultant erosion of the veridical self undermines the individual's sense of security. Where this results in clinical or sub-clinical depression it may culminate in suicide. The wounded self aims to both protect itself from residual erosion and offer a sacrifice to the public. Celebrity suicide often springs from feelings of contempt or hatred for the mass-media and fans. George Sanders, the character actor, killed himself by taking a drug overdose in 1972. His suicide note read 'Dear World: I am leaving because I am bored: I am leaving you with your worries in this sweet cesspool'. Kurt Cobain's suicide in 1994 followed drug problems and well-publicized complaints of feeling hounded by the public and the paparazzi. Marianne Faithfull's attempted suicide in 1969 followed Brian Jones's apparent death by misadventure in the same year. In her autobiography she sifts through her motives. In part, she reasons, taking a drug overdose was an act of revenge on other members of The Rolling Stones and the mass-media, whom she regarded as over-complacent about Jones's death. Faithfull identified with Jones, and she believed his death to have been a 'sacrifice'. Because the sacrifice failed to change the attitudes and behaviour of the group, the media and the fans, she decided that she must go one step further and really shock everyone. Her close identification with Jones – she refers to him as her 'twin' – is typical evidence of the veridical self's feelings of mortification or disappearance. According to her:

> From the age of seventeen until fairly recently, my life had been the life of a sleepwalker ... Managers, star-spotters, the press, the public. What they see in you might be who you really are, or it might be somebody else entirely. It doesn't matter; part of you falls asleep. The image with which you are imprinted is so indelible that it has the power to hypnotize you and those close to you ... In the struggle for my own direction, I began pushing everybody away, constantly saying: 'No, no, no' – to people, to situations and eventually to life itself. I am not this, I am not that, I am not the other. I always thought there was something wrong with me for not being happy with what I've got ... But sometimes it didn't feel like my life, it was as if I was living somebody else's.[11]

This section of Faithfull's memoir takes the form of a confession. Her suicide attempt was not cathartic. She did not abandon heroin use and, for a time, lived on the streets. However, in recognizing the factors involved in the gestation of her own personal disintegration, she identifies a surface in which it is possible to imagine personal reintegration. There is no abandonment of the public face, because wearing a 'front' is the inescapable condition of celebrity. At the same time, through public confession, she acknowledges a vulnerability that helps her to mediate her face in public without suffering from clinical or sub-clinical self-estrangement.

Paula Yates, the so-called 'Princess of Punk', died in September 2000, aged 40. The press reported that the police found empty vodka bottles, prescription drugs and heroin at her bedside, but no suicide note. In

Britain, Yates was the Punk Era's trademark mediagenic female reveller in outrage and publicity. Originally famous for being the celetoid girlfriend of Bob Geldof, Yates posed naked at the Reform Club for *Penthouse*, and published a book of photographs called *Rock Stars in their Underpants*. Eventually, she married Geldof and had three daughters with him. She also became a TV presenter. First she co-presented Channel 4's flagship '80s music show, *The Tube*. Later she worked as an interviewer for the *Big Breakfast* show, where her forté was to interview celebrities from a bed. One fateful interviewee was the INXS singer Michael Hutchence.

Yates cultivated a dizzy, voluptuous, flirtatious public image. This was temporarily softened in the mid-1980s when Geldof's Live Aid campaign to relieve Third World hunger projected her in the role of a co-humanitarian, and also by her proselytizing role as a celebrity mother. However, perhaps because of this, the media portrayed her affair with Michael Hutchence in 1995 as a scandal. Yates was used to being cast as an amoral wild child, but now she suffered the additional media taunt of being vilified as an irresponsible mother. Geldof won custody of the children, but eventually agreed to share the responsibility with Yates. In 1996 Hutchence and Yates became the parents of their own child, Heavenly Hiranni Tiger Lily. A year later, Hutchence died in bizarre circumstances. He was found hanging from a belt in a Sydney hotel room. Yates's despair seemed to be all-consuming. Her behaviour became increasingly erratic and volatile. She was treated for depression and fought an acrimonious custody battle over Tiger Lily with Hutchence's parents. She fiercely rejected the coroner's verdict that Hutchence's death was suicide. She insisted that it was a case of auto-erotic asphyxiation when a sexual game went tragically wrong.

In 1997 public revelations that her true father was Hughie Greene, the quiz show host of the 1960s and '70s, and not, as she believed, Jess Yates, a presenter of religious broadcasting, contributed to her fractured sense of self. Yates's public face was denigrated and publicly humiliated. Vilified by the media for leaving Geldof, she was assailed by the public judgement that

Hutchence had killed himself and hence, deliberately abandoned her. Now DNA tests questioned the authenticity of her veridical self. Bereft of a sense of origins and sundered from her lover in painful and ambiguous circumstances, her veridical self became increasingly embattled. In 1998 she was admitted to a psychiatric hospital, and two weeks later apparently tried to hang herself. She embarked on a series of well-publicized relationships, one with an ex-heroin addict who later sold his story to the newspapers. In 1999 she tried to relaunch her career by presenting *An Evening with Jerry Springer*, which flopped. *The Guardian*'s obituary (18 September 2000) listed her death as 'apparent suicide' (a premature, censorious judgement that was later refuted by the coroner's report), and concluded that 'She loved the spotlight, and her fame by association. Anonymity never suited her. She was vulgar, irrepressible and eccentric, and in many ways, represented all that is silly and vacuous about modern celebrity.'

The public confession is the medium through which the celebrity renegotiates a public face, following the acknowledgement of states of disintegration or near disintegration. Thus, Anthony Hopkins has regularly been interviewed about his fight against alcoholism and his Alcoholics Anonymous membership. Keith Richards is open about his former heroin addiction. Jim Bakker and Jimmy Lee Swaggart, the televangelists, both admitted extra-marital affairs and asked forgiveness from their tele-congregations. Swaggart, who confessed to consorting with a prostitute, begged for absolution on live TV from his wife, from his son, from the pastors and missionaries of his denomination and from his global followers. At the end of his public confession he turned to God: 'I have sinned against you, my Lord, and I would ask that your precious blood would wash and cleanse every stain until it is in the seas of God's forgetfulness, never to be remembered against me any more.' Bill Clinton also eventually, and after several public denials, confessed, in a TV broadcast to the nation, no less, that he did, despite all his previous denials, have sexual relations with Monica Lewinsky.

Celebrity homosexuality has a long history of being vigorously denied. Montgomery Clift, Terence Rattigan, Noel Coward, J. Edgar Hoover, John Gielgud and James Dean were all highly reticent about their sexuality. Liberace sued *The Daily Mirror* in 1956 for describing him as a 'sniggering, snuggling, scent-impregnated, quivering, fruit-flavoured, mincing heap of mother love'. Not unreasonably, Liberace claimed that the description imputed homosexuality. However he refuted the claim that he was a homosexual. Liberace remained in the closet until his death in 1987 from an AIDS-related illness, when he was posthumously outed by a coroner who insisted on an autopsy.

An interesting variant of the disintegration/confession nexus that has become quite prominent in recent years is the presentation of celebrity illness. Until quite recently, the presentation of serious, life-threatening celebrity illness was masked from the public. Physical disintegration following cancer, Alzheimer's disease or AIDS was hushed up until after death, or until the truth could no longer be disguised. The announcement that Ronald Reagan had Alzheimer's was delayed until his symptoms had made him a virtual recluse. The news that Michel Foucault, Ian Charleston, Anthony Perkins, Robert Fraser and Rudolf Nureyev had AIDS was only made public after their deaths. Rock Hudson, Freddie Mercury and Robert Mapplethorpe withheld the news that they were suffering from the illness until they were at death's door. This contrasts with other celebrities who were highly public about their condition. Derek Jarman, Oscar Moore, Kenny Everett, Magic Johnson, Holly Johnson and Harold Brodsky were very open about their HIV status. Indeed, Jarman became something of a crusader for raising public awareness about AIDS and combating hypocricy about gay lifestyle. Similarly, Frank Zappa announced that he was suffering from cancer early on in his illness. The playwright Dennis Potter agreed to a famous British TV interview with Melvyn Bragg in which he announced that he was suffering from terminal cancer, and spoke movingly about the illness and his imminent death. The journalists Ruth

Picardie, Martyn Harris and John Diamond all became national celebrities in the UK when they began to write newspaper columns about their own terminal cancer. Diamond's column in *The Times* left him with the unwelcome sobriquet of 'Mr Celebrity Cancer'.

This type of celebrity disintegration and confession does not derive from auto- or exo-degradation. Interestingly, and chillingly, Diamond revealed that he received emails and letters accusing him of being a narcissist in devoting a newspaper column to his illness and a class enemy in 'whingeing *ad infinitum*' about cancer of the tongue and throat while ignoring the 'true face of low-income disease'. But this form of exo-degradation in which diagnosis of class guilt, character weakness or personality defect is an element in the aetiology of the illness, is a negligible feature in the disintegration–confession nexus. Being open about celebrity terminal illness presents the celebrity in an out-of-face relationship with the public and ultimately reveals the resilience of the veridical self. The disintegration of the body produces a new surface on which the self coheres and continues in a different kind of dialogue with the public.

Redemption

Auto- and exo-degradation ceremonies traumatize the relationship between celebrities and their fans because they reveal a schism between the public face and the veridical self. Celebrities who openly show contempt for their fans and expose the public face as a mask run the risk of cultural disinvestment by the public. Both O. J. Simpson's murder trial and Gary Glitter's prison sentence for downloading child pornography from the internet had a devastating effect on their relationships with the public. So far, their attempts to repair the shattered chains of attraction by public interviews and confessions have failed.

Promiscuity in sexual relations, addiction to alcohol and narcotics or conspicuous consumption also degrades the idealized image of the celebrity in the eyes of the public. Fatty Arbuckle's career as a film comedian was destroyed in the early 1920s after he was tried for the manslaughter of the starlet Virginia Rappe. Arbuckle was acquitted, but he never escaped the taint of sexual perversity in connection with Rappe's death. Despite professing his innocence and trying to return to the screen, he was never again accepted by the public.

Louise Brooks, the scintillating silent star of *Pandora's Box* and *Diary of a Lost Girl* (both 1929), acquired the reputation for sexual libertinism, which resulted in the collapse of her career. Interestingly, Brooks was rediscovered by the English critic Kenneth Tynan in the 1970s living in obscurity and poverty. His profile revived public interest in her, both as a neglected icon of the 1920s and as a feminist heroine who had been punished for her sexual independence.

In 1994 Michael Jackson paid an undisclosed sum, believed to be over $25 million, to prevent the allegation that he sexually molested a thirteen-year-old boy being brought to trial. In interviews Jackson complained that he had been the victim of police intimidation and denied all charges. However, his position as the supreme idol of his day was seriously damaged.

But as the live TV broadcasts made by Jimmy Swaggart and Bill Clinton demonstrate, confession can indeed produce redemption. Redemption is the ritualized attempt by a fallen celebrity to re-acquire positive celebrity status through confession and the request for public absolution. In admitting to battles with alcoholism, Elizabeth Taylor, Richard Burton, Paul Merson, Tony Adams, Alex 'Hurricane' Higgins and George Best counterposed their idealized status with the public face of vulnerability. They appealed for compassion from the public rather than blind worship.

Redemption bids carry no guarantee of success. Political commentators usually agree that Clinton's confession and request for forgiveness over the Lewinsky affair hobbled his claim to be the moral leader of the nation. Curiously, for a nation that sets such outward store on cultural probity, Clinton's revelations did not fatally damage his position. His leadership of the longest bull market in postwar history deflected much of the criticism. He left the office of President in 2001 with the highest public approval ratings on record. Then again, he never regained the reputation of a 'Teflon President', one able to withstand moral taint. Clinton was branded as an amoral leader, an iconic status that fittingly summed up the hypocrisy and empty meretriciousness of the 1990s.

The fallen celebrity may never regain the former level of elevation in the public sphere. But confession can produce a more nuanced relationship with the public, in which frailty and vulnerability are recognized as the condition of embodiment, common to celebrity and fan alike. A sort of democracy is established between the celebrity and the fan on the basis of common embodiment, and the vulnerability that is the corollary of embodiment.

Redemption processes involve the active complicity of the audience. For fans are requested either to grant forgiveness in respect of personality weaknesses or negative behaviour that contrasts with the idealized image of the celebrity, or acknowledge the vulnerability and weakness of celebrity.

When Robert Downey Jnr was sentenced for drugs offences in 1999, an internet vigil was established. The 'To Know Him is To Love Him' website was run by 'lovers, friends and supporters' of the actor, and consisted of poems, letters and messages designed to keep him in the public eye. Downey claimed to have renounced drugs when he was released from the California State Penitentiary at Corcoran in August 2000. His drug use, and the prison sentence, made him a scandalous figure in Hollywood. However, his fan base remained substantially intact, thus increasing his chances of getting back into films. The point re-emphasizes the socially constructed character of celebrity. Redemption involves representational negotiation to restore the diminished cultural capital of the celebrity. In Downey's case, public sympathy was orchestrated by the website and a profile in *Vanity Fair* in which he expressed penitence. But the redemption script is high risk, since it acknowledges personality defects and depends on avoiding slipping back into the pattern of behaviour that provoked the public censure and punishment.

The Cult of Distraction

Celebrities are part of the culture of distraction today. Society requires distraction so as to deflect consciousness from both the fact of structured inequality and the meaninglessness of existence following the death of God. Religion provides a solution to the problem of structured inequality in this life by promising eternal salvation to true believers. With the death of God, and the decline of the Church, the sacramental props in the quest for salvation have been undermined. Celebrity and spectacle fill the vacuum. They contribute to the cult of distraction that valorizes the super-ficial, the gaudy, the domination of commodity culture. The cult of distraction is therefore designed to mask the disintegration of culture. Commodity culture is unable to produce integrated culture, because it brands each commodity as momentarily distinctive and ultimately replaceable. Likewise, celebrity culture cannot produce transcendent value because any gesture towards transcendence is ultimately co-opted by commodification.

Celebrity culture is a culture of faux ecstasy, since the passions it generates derive from staged authenticity rather than genuine forms of recognition and belonging. Materialism, and the revolt against material-ism, are the only possible responses. Neither is capable of engendering the unifying beliefs and practices relative to sacred things that are essential to religious belief. The cult of distraction, then, is both a means of concealing the meaninglessness of modern life and of reinforcing the power of commodity culture. Celebrity provides monumental images of elevation and magic. The psychological consequence of this is to enjoin us to adjust to our material circumstances and forget that life has no meaning. We adjust either by adopting the celebrity as a role model or colluding with the inference that the masses are obviously inferior to the gilded minority that occupy the pantheon of celebrity since they have not 'made it'. In each case there is a strong tendency to adopt celebrity style as a way of deflecting attention from the deeper, perhaps insoluble, questions about the proper content of life. On this account, celebrity culture produces an aestheticized reading of life that obscures material reality and, in particular, questions of social inequality and ethical justice.

The dichotomy concerning whether to regard celebrity culture as an energizing force or a stupefying one recurs throughout the literature. Arguably, it is a misleading dichotomy, leading to profitless debate. In every case, the social impact generated by a particular celebrity is a matter for empirical analysis. For example, it is not in serious dispute that Princess Diana's involvement in the landmines campaign dramatically raised public awareness of the issue and mobilized resources. Whether this outcome was the accomplishment of an essentially meretricious and self-serving personality is beside the point. The campaign helped to relieve suffering, and this relief could not have been accomplished so readily by other available means.

Celebrity Placement and Endorsement

Celebrities can indeed change things and fill us with powerful inclinations and cravings. This is one reason why celebrity endorsement is a sought-after feature in the market-place, and corporations will pay large sums to acquire it. The Nike advertising campaigns featuring Michael Jordan, Spike Lee and Bo Johnson in the late 1980s and early '90s dramatically increased sales. The Nike campaign slogan – *'Just do it'* – entered popular culture as a catch-phrase. In these examples, the economic and publicity effect of celebrity involvement can be measured quite precisely. What is less clear are the psychological, emotional and cultural motives that make people respond to celebrity campaigning and endorsement. Do we buy Nike because we desire to be associated with the physical prowess and power of Michael Jordan? Or do we have confidence in his personal veracity as a self-made athlete? Is Jordan's endorsement popular because he is a symbol of material success, with a bank balance most of us would envy? Or is the attraction more to do with Jordan's lifestyle, which is built around leisure and sport, whereas for most of the audience leisure and sport are available only *after* work? Was Jordan's playful, relaxed style a factor in suggesting that the Nike product is fun? His appeal in the Nike ads is probably a mixture of all these things.

Commodity placement operates on the principle that the public recognition of the celebrity as an admirable or desirable cultural presence can be transferred onto the commodity in a commercial or ad. The cultural impact of placement depends on the condensation of associations in the consciousness of spectators around an overwhelming image that the celebrity confers positive value. The Coors and Hershey advertising campaigns of the 1980s used retro Pop culture to advertise their product. Images of Neil Armstrong on the moon, Elvis Presley, Marilyn Monroe and Sugar Ray Leonard were presented as 'American Originals'. The re-mythologizing of American Pop culture was used as the lever to mythologize the commodity. In the late 1990s, Apple used billboard images of John Lennon and Yoko Ono, Gandhi, Orson Welles, Alfred Hitchcock, Albert Einstein and other celebrity mavericks in the 'Think Different' campaign to suggest the unique cachet conferred by possessing an Apple computer.

The examples illustrate the complexity of the relationship between mass desire and celebrity status. We are drawn to celebrities for a variety of reasons. These can only be concretely established through empirical investigation. At the level of theory, it might be hypothesized, *inter alia*, that celebrities provide us with heroic role models in an age of mass standardization and predictability. They are idealized sexual objects who present an intense sexuality that is designed to attract us but, at the same time, to withhold consummation. They express human vulnerability and frailty that engages our sympathy and respect, and which also, perhaps, sets a standard of physical and mental decomposition that exerts a cautionary influence in the management of emotions in daily life. They are symbols of material success, and in flaunting the prodigious surplus given to them they are, at one and the same time, magnets of desire, envy and disapproval. In addition, notoriety allows society to present disturbing and general social tendencies as the dislocated, anti-social behaviour of folk demons. Mass murderers like Timothy McVeigh and serial killers like Fred and Rosemary West and Harold Shipman are presented by the mass-media as isolated figures in a macabre theatre of horror. Arguably, their notorious celebrity distracts us from facing the eternal questions concerning life, death and the meaning of existence. By distracting us from the terror of realizing that existence is ultimately meaningless, it might be argued that celebrities perform a significant therapeutic function in contemporary culture. However, because this function is not typically organized or planned in any rigorous or binding way, it is more plausible to regard it as a by-product of a wider cult of materialism in which the purpose of distraction is to accumulate value for the celebrity. The idea that celebrity culture is a means of cultural displacement, in which the loneliness of existence is compensated for by the illusion of recognition and belonging, is certainly at the heart of Structuralist readings that equate celebrity culture with social control and economic exploitation. But do these readings adequately explain the extraordinary prodigality of celebrity culture in contemporary society?

The Prodigality of Celebrity Culture

The shaman in tribal society is either a singular figure or part of a small group defined by ancestral bloodline or bio-cultural stigmata. His role is constrained by inherited beliefs and rituals and his influence is culturally synchronized to become pre-eminent in relation to cyclical or ceremonial requirements. At feast-time, war, birth, mourning and burial, the shaman's power is ascendant. At other times it is an understated, immanent element in the life of the tribe.

In contrast, celebrities are relatively profuse in modern society, and their presence is ubiquitous. It is not merely a question of the manifold ranks of celebrity relating to sport, music, art, film, literature, humanitarianism, politics and the other institutions of modern culture. Within these ranks, upward and downward mobility is a continuous characteristic of the status hierarchy to which celebrity watchers, and the general public, are perpetually attuned. In addition, the mass-media supply a diet of celetoids and celeactors to the public. The very prodigality of celebrity culture in contemporary society suggests an absence.

It might be thought, as Structuralists do, that the cause of this absence is materialism. The desire for wealth creates an overheated culture in which celebrities are constructed as commodities for economic accumulation. The celebrity race is very obviously bound up with the desire for wealth. But material explanations alone cannot explain the prodigality of celebrity in modern culture. After all, celebrity performers do not stop performing after they become millionaires. Michael Caine, Sean Connery, Jack Nicholson, Clint Eastwood, Tina Turner, Joni Mitchell, Barry White, Eric Clapton, Keith Richards, Elton John, Mick Jagger and Neil Young are sufficiently rich never to have to work again. Greed alone is not a sufficient motive to explain their readiness to devote much of their fifties and beyond to performing. Yet while they may now pace themselves more carefully, they do not retire from the screen or stage. Public acclaim answers to a deep psychological need in all of us for recognition. Acclaim carries the sensual pleasure of being acknowledged as an object of desire and approval.

Despite external appearances, celebrities are perhaps among the most insecure people in our midst. Their appeal is certainly a measure of our own insecurity. The original condition of being in the world is openness. This is the cause of our vulnerability and our desire to impose control. Being in the world is always socially interconnected. Hence there is an inherent tension between being and society, for we can never be entirely comfortable in a world where the satisfaction of our desires depends on others, and where the principles of scarcity and human vulnerability pattern our actions and responses. The sociological attempt to integrate being and society around ideology or hegemony is inadequate, for it presents a one-dimensional view of openness in which, for example, being is understood as the reflection of corporate power, the culture industry, capital, the state, patriarchy, money culture or an equivalent directing agency. On this reading, a significant function of celebrity is to enable us to manage vulnerability and cope with the fact of our own mortality.

Certainly the dilemma of vulnerability and immortality is accentuated in 'post-God' societies. The death of God is the original end of the unifying recognition that we live under one ideological system. Henceforward, the differentiation of taste and the pluralization of culture become more pronounced in the public sphere. In the absence of a unifying deity, some people search for cult figures to give life new meaning. From the particularity of a cultural position, universal claims are often made. It is unsatisfactory to view celebrities only as objects of control and manipulation. They are also symbols of belonging and recognition that distract us in positive ways from the terrifying meaninglessness of life in a post-God world. Our desire for distraction makes us peculiarly vulnerable to shamanism.

Both Charles Manson and Jim Jones exerted hypnotic power over their disciples. Manson was the ringleader behind the murders of Sharon Tate and other celebrities in Hollywood in 1969. Jones was the eponymous head of Jonestown, a religious community in Guyana, who ordered his flock of 913 to commit 'revolutionary suicide' in 1978. More recently, David Koresh was the inspirational leader at the centre of the Waco massacre. Shoko Asahara was the figurehead of the Aum Shinrikyo ('Supreme Truth') movement in Japan, who was found guilty of unleashing sarin nerve gas at Matsumoto city in 1994, killing seven people and injuring 144 others, and in the Tokyo subway system in 1995, killing twelve and injuring thousands. In 2000, at the Ugandan settlements of Rugazi, Buhunga, Roshojwa and Kanungu, the remains of over 900 people were exhumed. The dead were recovered from the headquarters of the 'Movement for the Restoration of the Ten Commandments of God'. They were the victims of a sect headed by Joseph Kibwetere, Father Dominic Kataribabo and a former prostitute, Credonia Mwerinde. The millennarian 'Movement' predicted the end of the world on the last day of the twentieth century. The sect members were prophesized to be rescued by 'a chariot of fire sent by the Lord'. When the prophecy failed, the congregation grew restive, and Mwerinde postponed the date of deliverance until March. At the time of writing, the subsequent pattern of events remains unclear. Newspaper reports suggest that 400 cult followers may have been executed, and a further 550 immolated themselves at the behest of their leaders.

The success of televangelism in the USA is further evidence of the persistence of religious belief. However, without seeking to mitigate the significance of evangelicals, fundamentalists and pentecostals in America's culture and economy, their public profile exaggerates their power. Their prominence is a symptom of the relative decline of the mainstream churches. The theatricality and emotionalism of Jimmy Swaggart and Pat Robertson draws on the folk tradition of evangelism in America. But televangelism is also an extension of the mass-media, and employs the basic devices of elevation and magic that are integral to celebrity culture.

Celebrity culture is inherently inflationary. For the impetus is always on being bigger and brighter. Organized religion has itself succumbed to this tendency. By 1995 Pope John Paul II had canonized 276 saints and beatified 768 people. This is more than all the other twentieth-century popes combined. Jean Paul II's world tours, with the ritual kissing of the soil on alighting from his aircraft, and the staged authenticity of mass rallies and live TV links, clearly borrow many of the ceremonies and devices refined by Hollywood and the rock industry for the presentation of celebrity to the public.

Celebrity culture is no substitute for religion. Rather, it is the milieu in which religious recognition and belonging are now enacted. That this milieu has adapted ceremonies of ascent and descent that were prefigured in religion is beside the point. The ubiquity of the milieu is the real issue. Today perhaps only the family rivals celebrity culture in providing the scripts, prompts and supporting equipment of 'impression management' for the presentation of self in public life. Indeed, a good deal of evidence, notably the high rate of divorce and the rising number of single-person households, suggests that the family is in decline, while celebrity culture seems to be triumphantly ascendant.

The desire to be recognized as special or unique is perhaps an inevitable feature of cultures built around the ethic of individualism. The overwhelming desire for ordinary people to be validated as stars is, arguably, part of the modern psychopathology of everyday life, and is significant only in the age of celebrity culture. For example, Jennifer Ringley, an otherwise 'ordinary' person, has constructed a website that consists of scenes from her daily life – eating, reading, talking to friends and sleeping. Her sex life is not shown. In 1998 her site was receiving over 500,000 hits daily.

Some years ago Christopher Lasch argued that the 'cult of narcissism' permeates contemporary culture.[12] The narcissistic personality lives in a condition dominated by self-absorption, in which psychic and social relevance is focused on the practices and wants of the self rather than on the state of society. Narcissism is associated with the hyper-inflation of the ordinary. The musings and experiences of a housewife, an office worker, a student – ordinary people – are invested with cosmic significance. Lasch had in mind the spread of popular psychology and psychic self-help programmes in the late 1960s and '70s.

Ringley's website is an extension of the cult of narcissism. It presupposes not only that a mass audience will find the monotonous, predictable existence of an ordinary person interesting, but that regularly following this routine produces social cohesion. To begin with, spectators are perhaps drawn to the site for voyeuristic reasons. It offers a keyhole into the private existence of someone else. But voyeurism is an insufficient reason to explain the longevity and popularity of the site. In addition the website offers repeated opportunities for identification and recognition. By entering the site regularly, spectators establish a routine in their own lives that is the basis for filling the void of loneliness.

In this chapter I have questioned whether celebrity culture has replaced religion as the focus of recognition and belonging. I submit that the rites of ascent and descent that were originally developed in primitive religion have been taken over and recast by celebrity culture. This is not, however, a one-way process. Organized religion has borrowed some of the forms and styles of retailing and mass communication perfected in the organization of celebrity in public life. Disneyland has been used as a stage for religious recruitment, and Pope John Paul II has turned some aspects of the papal dispensation of sainthood into an Oscar ceremony. I have also submitted that convergence is not total. Organized religion remains committed to producing a general view of social and spiritual order. Celebrity culture motivates intense emotions of identification and devotion, but it is basically a fragmented, unstable culture that is unable to sustain an encompassing, grounded view of social and spiritual order. None the less, some elements of celebrity culture do have a sacred significance for spectators. To the extent that organized religion has declined in the West, celebrity culture has emerged as one of the replacement strategies that promote new orders of meaning and solidarity. As such, notwithstanding the role that some celebrities have played in destabilizing order, celebrity culture is a significant institution in the normative achievement of social integration.

CHAPTER THREE

Celebrity and Aestheticization

In the last year of his life, the lawyer and gastronome Jean-Anthelme Brillat-Savarin (1755–1826) published *The Physiology of Taste*, a book on the aesthetics of dining that has since become famous. For Brillat-Savarin, 'taste' – aesthetic appreciation – was an attribute of 'the sensitive ego', and a sign of cultivation and refinement. He based his argument on an evolutionary principle that supposed the sensations of early man 'were absolutely direct, that is to say, that he saw without precision, heard without clarity, ate without discernment, and made love without tenderness'. But over time,

> since all of these sensations have a common centre in the soul, the special attribute of mankind and the ever active cause of perfectibility, they were considered, compared, and judged in the soul; and soon all the senses were led to help one another, for the use and benefit of the *sensitive ego*, or, to call it by another name, *the individual*.

The notion that taste is a quality of 'the sensitive ego', is no longer novel. However, Brillat-Savarin's proposition, that the acme of taste is available to all, assumed the crystallization of a new form of social order in which standards of taste were no longer divided between Court and society, but instead permeated society, and emerged and changed from within its midst.

Taste is, of course, pivotal in celebrity culture. Indeed, the growth of celebrity culture is closely bound up with the aestheticization of everyday life. The German philosopher Alexander Baumgarten coined the term *aesthetics* in the 1750s. Aesthetics refers to the enquiry into the nature and perception of beauty. In the Enlightenment, taste was developed as one of the principal categories for measuring progress. Kant held that a theory of beauty is on a par with a theory of truth and goodness. Taste distinguished humans from the animal world and set the civilized person apart from the savage. It was essential in assigning honour and respect to others, and in claiming them for oneself.

Taste became a mark of recognition in which individuals acknowledged solidarity in regard to specific cultural mores and values. Groupings of fans in celebrity culture can be regarded as taste cultures, cultivating and refining standards of emulation and solidarity in respect of the celebrity to whom they are attached.

The aestheticization of everyday life refers to the process by which perception and judgement regarding beauty and desire become generalized in the course of habitual exchange. The public mode of being is elaborated through new body idioms, criteria of personal noteworthiness and styles of behaviour. Urbanization, and the expansion of mass communication, enhance personal consciousness of co-presence. The growth of celebrity accompanied the expansive rise of public society. The emergence of print cultures, at first local, but quite rapidly national and global in their sphere of influence, was crucial in the development of public opinion.

At first, the public face is developed as a mechanism for managing social interaction. Erving Goffman demonstrated that the public face assumes an 'interaction tonus', or pitch, through which responsiveness to social encounters is maintained. Facial muscles, hair, make-up and clothing establish a personal front that conveys social competence. The absence of these characteristics implies a lack of self-discipline and, concomitantly, inferior social skills. Neglect of personal appearance and hygiene are typical signs of incipient psychopathology. A man of note is defined by his appearance, speech and opinions. All of these qualities contribute to the cachet of the individual, the impact he or she exerts over the public. Because celebrity in contemporary society is a version of self-presentation, it is important to elucidate the history of the public face. This history is related to the development of new technologies of communication, especially photography, but it is also part of new ways of relating to strangers and promoting the self that accompany mass urbanization, commodification and industrialization.

The Rise of the Public Face

In the eighteenth century, the elaboration of the public face was exposed to new behaviour-setting regimes. The explosion of print culture multiplied the means of communication through which taste cultures were nurtured and refined. It is not enough to assert this; one must also briefly elucidate the pace and scale of transformation, for example in England. Before 1700, almost no printing presses were licensed in the English provinces. Newspapers, periodicals and books were printed in London and spread, somewhat laboriously, to the country via the coaching service. But in the eighteenth century the provincial press expanded rapidly. The *Norwich Post* began in 1701, the *Bristol Postboy* in 1702, and by the end of the century nearly every major town boasted at least one local newspaper. In London, by contrast, in 1790 no less than fourteen morning papers were on sale across the capital.[1] Later, in the nineteenth century, a clear bifurcation in the press occurred between papers concentrating on 'news', preferably 'sensational' or 'sensation-making', and those concerned with serious, 'objective' commentary. The first celetoids emerged in papers concentrating on news and sensation.

The liberalization of printing licences swelled the production of engravings, pamphlets, cartoons and ballads. Magazines such as *The Spectator*, *The Gentleman's Magazine*, *Matrimonial Magazine* and *The Westminster* were founded, and communicated channels of news, information and opinion that was crucial in the formation of national–popular, and later global, taste cultures. The ubiquity of print culture increased the representation of ideas, reputations and images of public figures. Through cartoons and caricatures it also provided a mechanism for distorting reputation and inflecting the public face for satirical purposes.

Novels and histories also began to achieve mass circulation, thus spreading ideas and reputations and introducing the first celeactors into popular culture. Fictional characters like Lemuel Gulliver, Robinson Crusoe, Tom Jones and Tristram Shandy began to populate popular discourse, and their fictional life and opinions inscribed themselves on the public. The speed and extent of this process must be kept in proportion. The price of books remained high, and literacy was far from universal. The educated – usually rich or well-off in metropolitan centres like London, Bristol and Liverpool – constituted the reading class of the day. None the less, in 1742 Henry Fielding's *Joseph Andrews* sold 6,500 copies. Publishers tackled the high cost of producing books by releasing them in serial form. Thus, Smollett's *History of England* sold 13,000 copies. Pattern-books, for example John Wood's *Series of Plans for Cottages*, and magazines such as *The Gallery of Fashion* and *The Fashions of London and Paris* supplied readers with new aesthetic criteria.

In short, the eighteenth century established national–popular and global mass audiences, and celebrities for those audiences. Crucially, this was absent from earlier social formations that were only capable of producing *pre-figurative* forms of celebrity. Of course, the construction of the public face in the eighteenth century continued to make use of local materials supplied by family and community. But this now operated in a more elaborate, multi-layered context, in which data, opinions and advice on public presentation were supplied by people spatially remote from spectators and consumers. The division between the veridical self and the public face became more pronounced and elaborate. Achieved notability and notoriety became objects of public debate and opinion. Ordinary individuals began to measure themselves against achieved celebrities, especially after the American and French Revolutions, in which ascribed celebrity was attacked and ridiculed. As democracy and commodification spread, people began to accumulate role models, expressions, styles of dress and opinions from print culture. Newspaper and magazine proprietors, ever conscious of being locked into a ratings war, prevailed on their editors to supply newsworthy events and figures for a ravenous public. The celetoid is the product of the age of para-social relations, which boomed in the eighteenth century.

Arguably, the chains of power binding a leader to society were always primarily symbolic, so that para-social relations are part and parcel of all systems of mass government. For example, Julius Caesar, Augustus and other leaders dominated life in Ancient Rome, but typically they remained physically remote from the daily experience of most Romans. Similarly, under Christianity, Jesus was worshipped as the 'light of the world', yet as the resurrected son of God, his physical presence was absent from the earth.

However, in the eighteenth century the separation between celebrities and spectators was attenuated through print culture. Newspapers and magazines rapidly adopted a distinctive public tone that was personally accented so as to convey independence. Because the mass-media were situated in a competitive market, the personal quality of newspapers and magazines developed through infighting and status wars. Public culture, in as much as it was expressed in the mass-media, became a culture of attitudes struck, opinions exchanged and stands taken. The mode of communication provided unprecedented opportunities for role-playing, role reversal and, of course, the expansion of the public imagination in respect of the dimensions and contradictions of achieved celebrity. Gradually, personal value became affixed to calculated, external appearance. Marx argued that the rise of capitalism involved the transition from use values to exchange values as the normal mode of social and economic interaction. This presupposed aestheticization, since it maintained that the external appearance and design of commodities acquires more significance as exchange value becomes generalized.

Although Marx wrote primarily about the commodity, the same observation applies to the body. In societies dominated by exchange value, the idiom and image of bodily presentation increases in economic and social importance. Being attractive and able to manufacture desire become sought-after attributes in the market. The body ceases to be merely the locus of desire, it becomes the facade through which distinction and attraction are registered. In as much as this is so, the body becomes a commodity. That is, not strictly speaking a personal possession, but an object of consumption, designed and packaged to generate desire in others and achieve impact in public.

It was no accident, therefore, that fashion became more pronounced in eighteenth-century English culture. Of course, Tudor, Elizabethan and Jacobean cultures had fathered their bucks and dandies. But only in the eighteenth century did fashion celebrities emerge from the ranks of Court society to influence opinion and taste in the whole of public society. For example, George Bryan, more popularly known as the Regency dandy Beau Brummell, achieved celebrity through manipulating fashion and taste. Brummell's extravagant fastidiousness with dress and make-up was in part a reaction to the *citoyen* simplicity of French Revolutionaries and the gaudy costume of the seventeenth-century fop. Contrary to popular impression today, Brummell's style of dress was characterized by austerity. The public face that he sought to cultivate was concerned with achieving concentrated propriety in public appearance, and defining a public face against the standards of excess and waste associated with the aristocracy. But it also reflected the growing importance of fashion and Romantic self-absorption as insignia of status and value. Although Brummell's influence depended decisively on his friendship with the Prince of Wales (later George IV), his celebrity demonstrated the new susceptibility of public culture to trend-setting initiatives from the midst of society rather than from the Court.

Fashion is conventionally associated with social membership. Mary Douglas argued that body modification by means such as tattooing, piercing and painting is a metaphor of the social body.[2] Through bodily adornment and modification, the individual enlarges the impression of his or her personality and expresses cultural solidarity. At the start of the twentieth century, the sociologist Georg Simmel proposed that adornment and fashion contribute to what he termed the 'radioactivity' of the individual.[3] In the eighteenth century, fashion became a more prominent marker of cultural capital. In becoming more prominent, it also became more differentiated, since individuals began to compete more intensively with one another to impress others with aesthetic impact and body culture. Sartorial appearance became a more significant feature of life strategy, since it conveyed immediately a facade of coherent lifestyle values and aspirations.

The growth of aestheticization in the eighteenth century was, however, founded on a paradox. As the sources and channels of data and opinion formation multiplied, as para-social interaction became normalized, the public relationships between people became more anonymous. Consider Tom Paine's book, *Common Sense* (1776), perhaps the key document of the American Revolution. *Common Sense* was not, of course, the first book to sue for the political transformation of society. Sir Thomas More's *Utopia* (1516) had sketched a communist society, and Gerard Winstanley's *The Law of Freedom* (1651) outlined the principles for a society based on equality, cooperation and a secular humanist ethic. More's discussion was defused by what Christopher Hill has called the writer's *jeu d'esprit*, Winstanley's pamphlet achieved a local, uneven impact among the working-class. Paine's *Common Sense*, in contrast, was a publishing phenomenon. Paine himself estimated that over 120,000 copies were published in America within six months, and the book also circulated widely in Europe. Paine became the most celebrated ideologist of the American Revolution, and was acknowledged as such for the rest of his long, turbulent and fascinating life.[4] On his return to his native Britain, radical groups fêted him by holding banquets and celebrations in his honour. Paine wrote *The Rights of Man* (1791) in London during an extended stay at Islington's The Angel Inn as his rebuttal to Edmund Burke's polemic against the French Revolution. It broke all publishing records. In 1791 the average size of a print-run was 1,250 copies for a novel and 750 for more general books. Even at the high price of three shillings (the publisher's decision), the book sold 50,000 copies in two months. In 1791 the population of Britain was around ten million, of which perhaps 40 per cent were literate. Paine later estimated that within ten years in Britain alone, sales of the complete, unabridged edition reached somewhere between 400,000 and half a million. After the Bible, it was the most widely read book of all time in any language. Not only that, for *The Rights of Man* was regularly read aloud, thus increasing the spread of its arguments and the fame, and later, notoriety of Paine's name.

The success and impact of Paine's books, both of which openly criticize established government and encourage revolution, reflect the advances made in the liberalization of information and opinion. In the seventeenth century, government censors and the Stationers' Company restricted the flow of incendiary books and pamphlets by licensing and policing. Although they were unable to prevent commercially minded pirates from printing and distributing illicit texts, they constituted a considerable barrier against free speech expressed in writing. By the early eighteenth century it became increasingly difficult to enforce this type of centralized control over print. True, in 1792 William Pitt's government, alarmed by the popularity of Paine's book, which attacked the hereditary principle of government in Britain and praised the French Revolution, issued a proclamation against seditious writings. Government spies and officials engaged in a campaign of harassment that eventually forced Paine to flee to Paris. Pitt's tactics labelled Paine as a seditious character, which only served to enhance his celebrity status among radicals. As a short-stop gain, it achieved Paine's ejection from his homeland. But it failed to prevent the book from continuing to circulate. The concentration of populations in urban centres encouraged the growth of literacy, and this, combined with the improvement in transport achieved by the growth of the coach and canal systems, facilitated communication. Radical thought could no longer be confined in the state straitjacket of the Puritan era. Printing-presses could not be effectively silenced by government proclamation or decree.

The physical anonymity of writers and pundits in print culture was extremely propitious to the emergence of celebrity culture. The elevation of celebrities via books, pamphlets and newspaper articles provided innumerable reference points and role models for recognition, belonging and emulation. Celebrity culture embodied desire, and therefore went some way towards correcting the anonymity of habitual public relationships. It articulated aspirations, inner wants and cravings. Yet precisely because celebrities were generally linked to spectators by long chains of attraction, celebrity culture vastly increased the significance of para-social interaction in culture. The connection between celebrities and fans is overwhelmingly an imaginary relationship. The content of the relationship is unquestionably shaped by business interests, and the consequences of the relationship for both celebrities and fans may run deep, but unconscious and subconscious desire is at the heart of the matter. In the eighteenth century the means of embodying and communicating desire changed decisively. Before coming to the nature of this change, and illustrating its significance through a short analysis of transformations in the English theatre, it is necessary to go into more detail about the relation of unconscious and subconscious desire to celebrity culture.

One might posit that celebrities are, in part, the projection and articulation of unconscious and subconscious desire. The public face of the celebrity contains traces of wishes and fantasies that are ubiquitous in popular culture. The subconscious desire for heroes, ecstatic experience and transgression is symbolically accommodated by the para-social relations propagated by celebrity culture. Notable and notorious celebrities are the result. Structuralist approaches to celebrity stress the determined nature of these wishes and fantasies, and identify commerce as the primary agent of manipulation. Without wishing to underrate the relevance of this perspective, it is perhaps necessary to insist on what one might term the surplus vitality of unconscious and subconscious desire. Thus, para-social interaction is the adjunct of generalized, reciprocal relations in which episodic, fragmentary contact between anonymous actors is pre-eminent. In ordinary life we encounter the calculated assembly of body culture. The police, the magistrate, the shopkeeper, no less than the criminal, the prostitute and the confidence man, present a public face to the world, but this face disguises the veridical self. Unconscious and subconscious desires and fantasies in respect of the true state of other people's veridical selves is the inevitable condition of this state of affairs.

In the eighteenth century the prerequisites for global types of para-social interaction, if one may put it like this, fell into place. The notion of a person simultaneously 'out front' and 'in disguise' became the common currency of cultural interaction. Of course, the eighteenth century did not invent this distinction. Machiavelli's analysis in *The Prince* (1513) provided a veritable manual for the techniques of dissembling the veridical self. But it was not until the eighteenth century that new mechanisms of print communication combined with the rapid expansion of urban populations, the growth of literacy, the commercialization of culture and the changing balance of power between Court and society to make textual data genuine practical guides for self help.

The proliferation of affordable texts, which reflected changing mores and opinions, projected embodiment and aesthetics to the centre of ordinary social interaction. Aestheticization did not necessarily make life more beautiful. Commodity design, and designs for living, were part of the same process of capitalist expansion. This process required the commodity to fill the universe of consumer culture, leaving no nook or cranny vacant. This often produced a coarsening of taste as entrepreneurs vied with each other for new forms of advertising and entertainment that would attract the masses. The nineteenth century, which gave the world the exquisite aesthetics of John Ruskin, A.W.N. Pugin, Henry Cole and William Morris, also produced P. T. Barnum and the peep show. But these developments, and the subsequent course of popular culture, were built on foundations of communication and taste laid down in the eighteenth century.

Why did aesthetics and styles of embodiment become pronounced in eighteenth-century culture? John Brewer's recent study of the popularization of taste argues that, in the century between the 1660s and 1760s, taste cultures multiplied in European society.[5] The growth of industry and the increasing concentration of urban populations were crucial factors in effecting change. So were the technological innovations in the various branches of the arts and sciences. However, the crux of the multiplication of taste cultures was the shifting balance of power between the Court and society. Royal patronage was not erased during this period. Indeed, the Court influenced popular culture well into the twentieth century. Yet, the eighteenth century sowed the seeds of the irreversible decline in the Court's influence. Royal patronage was supplanted by the new taste cultures emerging in the coffee-houses, reading societies, debating clubs, assembly rooms, galleries and concert halls. The origins of celebrity culture are rooted in this great transformation. From it, demotic taste cultures, developing varied and diverse standards of taste, emerged. In addition, the business of satisfying these taste cultures and expanding them became one of the specialized, and most lucrative, objects of commerce.

Of course, in ancient times achieved celebrity was not unknown: individuals on occasion did rise to prominence from the lower ranks. The Athenian stage produced famous actors, for example Thespis of Icaria, who won the first Tragedy contest in 535 BC. Cicero rose from the class of landowners and bankers to dominate aristocratic society in Rome. He was said to have learnt his powers of oration from the celebrated actor Quintus Roscius and the tragedian Aesop. But it was comparatively rare for ordinary men and women to capture the public imagination. *Ascribed* celebrity dominated, and the social order of the time developed ways of monitoring and policing the ranks of achieved celebrity to ensure they posed no threat to the continuance of the time-worn distribution of power.

The Theatre in England

How, then, was the popularization of taste cultures, and the emergence of celebrity cultures in which *achieved* celebrity plays the pre-eminent role, accomplished? The history of the theatre in England gives some insight into the eddies and flows of the process. Because the theatre is concerned with presentation and projection, it has been an important laboratory in the evolution of the rhetorical, didactic, sexual and comedic repertory of the public face. From pre-Roman times, itinerant popular entertainers like dancers, mimes, minstrels and storytellers figured in the oral tradition. Folk plays developed from seasonal celebrations and mimetic elements in dance. Many of these were fused with the Church's liturgical calendar. The Middle Ages witnessed a growing taste for civic pageantry and 'mystery plays' (biblical histories portrayed on fixed stages). Liturgical dramas began to be eclipsed by secular morality plays. Professional touring companies, mummings and disguisings started to receive aristocratic patronage. The establishment of the royal household post of Master of the Revels in

1494 both legitimized the theatre and created a central mechanism for regulating the content of performances.

In the sixteenth century the tradition of strolling players performing in the yards of inns or in private banqueting halls expanded. The growth and concentration of the population in London intensified the popular demand for permanent playhouses. The actor-manager James Burbage, who originally trained as an artisan joiner, opened the first public theatre at Shoreditch in 1576. It was quickly followed by the Rose (1587), the Swan (1595) and the Globe (1599) at Bankside; the Fortune (1600) at Cripplegate; the Red Bull (1614); and the Hope (1614), again at Bankside. The establishment of the theatre in London created the conditions for actors and playwrights to achieve public repute. The greatest dramatist of the period was, of course, William Shakespeare, but Christopher Marlowe and Ben Jonson were also celebrated public figures. However, more prestige was vested in being an actor than a playwright. So, in their day, players like Richard Tarlton, known as the greatest clown of the Elizabethan age, Edward Alleyn, Will Kempe, John Hemmings and Richard Burbage were all better-known celebrities. In taking the monarchy as a subject for dramatic histories and tragedies, Elizabethan and Jacobean playwrights exposed the foibles, vanities and weaknesses of Court society. Indeed, the theatre of the time was remarkable in using drama to criticize the whole panoply of ascribed celebrity. Because of this, it was also the target of Puritans and Royalists, who called for more restraint in the criticism of public figures.

The *Ordinance Against Stage Plays*, passed at the outbreak of the Civil War in 1642, closed down public theatres. However, although it brought the curtain down on public performances, it failed to extinguish the dramatic tradition. The theatre was forced underground. After the Restoration in 1660, public theatre was revived as a legitimate public entertainment. Charles II issued two patents, to Sir Thomas Killigrew and Sir William Davenant, which granted a monopoly of performed drama in

London until 1843. Killigrew created the King's Company and performed plays at Gibbon's Tennis Court, and later Drury Lane. Davenant formed the Duke's Company and performed at Lincoln's Inn Fields and, later, at Covent Garden. Initially, the forté of both companies was the revival, and surgical transformation, of old plays. But the new companies also developed their own style of entertainment, dominated by a new genre, the Comedy of Manners. The audience for such plays, by Wycherley, Congreve, Vanbrugh, Farquhar and others, was not the popular one of Shakespeare's day, but a more fashionable one that, in many ways, regarded the theatre as an extension of Court society.

A notable feature of Restoration theatre is that for the first time it permitted women to act on the stage. Elizabeth Barry, Rebecca Marshall, Anne Bracegirdle, Frances Maria Knight, Mary Lee and others gained considerable public acclaim, but the celebrity achieved by their male counterparts – Colley Cibber, Thomas Betterton, Thomas Doggett, Henry Harris – was always greater. The prejudice against female involvement carried over in the treatment of actresses as secondary players in the theatrical pecking order.

The 1737 Licensing Act confirmed the monopoly of the two patent theatres at Drury Lane and Covent Garden, authorized the Lord Chamberlain to act as censor and restricted the development of non-licensed playhouses. However, the growth of urban–industrial society had already exceeded the limits of effective Court control. The appetite for a theatre of ideas and sarcastic burlesque produced informal, mobile street theatre, in which drama, dance, farce, pantomime and songs predominated. The growth of the population in provincial towns revived and expanded the tradition of travelling troupes of players. David Garrick, the most celebrated actor-manager of the eighteenth century, learned his craft in such company. Garrick developed a naturalistic acting style, refined the notion of a theatrical canon focused on the plays of Shakespeare and assiduously presented himself as a public figure, a model actor-manager whose taste and discernment regarding the canon was on a par with the leading literary critics of the day. Because print culture had extended greatly between the sixteenth and eighteenth centuries, the prominence of the stage in national life was vastly enhanced. Garrick himself became one of the towering celebrities of the age. A connoisseur of the arts, a gourmand and an impeccable gentleman, he was lionized by the aristocracy and popularly regarded as a national treasure.

Garrick travelled in select circles. None the less, it would be a mistake to infer that his success is evidence that the division between Court and society had completely fallen away. For all his achievements in establishing a classical repertory for the English theatre, and glorifying the spoken tradition of English, Garrick, whose theatre was essentially a stage in which high culture was self-consciously reinvented and venerated, remained fairly peripheral to the key levers of power. So long as he conformed to the standards of respectability of his day and avoided scandal, he was accepted by polite society. But the welcome he received was conditional, and he never moved from the fringes of wealth, power and influence. Artistic licence was embroidered with the caveats of established power. The poverty and neglect suffered by Mozart in Vienna demonstrated the fate of artists when the taint of scandal turned the Court against them. Nearly two centuries were to elapse before artists could be open about their sexuality, religious beliefs and politics without fearing that candour would damage their careers.

In the nineteenth century the public was presented with new forms of popular amusement that contrasted pointedly with Garrick's theatre of high culture. Burford's Panorama in Leicester Square offered new visual wonders, while the rise of the music-hall and tavern culture presented new, intimate venues for burlesque and tragedy. The Theatre Regulation Act of 1834 broke the monopoly of Drury Lane and Covent Garden. Although censorship was not abolished until 1968, the English theatre slowly became more challenging by tackling social and political issues. Oscar Wilde's drawing-room comedies at the end of the century actually ridiculed the mores and prejudices of upper-class life, but Wilde was always more interested in aesthetics than politics, so his dramatic work never developed into a truly critical theatre. However, by 1900 the path to the socially critical, class-sensitive, kitchen-sink dramas of the 1950s and '60s, explored in the work of John Osborne, Harold Pinter and David Mercer, was already being cleared.

The development of the theatre in England illustrates the central processes involved in the aestheticization of everyday life. At the outset, the monopoly of taste exercised by the Court was broken and taste cultures multiplied through the growth of industry, commerce, travel and the increasing urban concentration of populations. In time, taste cultures expanded from local and national to global levels. Print culture – and later the electronic mass-media – extended the chains of attraction between celebrities and fans over huge distances and in manifold ways. Desire became fixated on physically absent objects and therefore assumed an abstract quality. Representation, and the various industries of media repre-sentation, developed into the passport for celebrity recognition. As achieved celebrity displaced ascribed celebrity, the enlargement of the public sphere and the relaxation of coercive centralized standards intensi-fied and magnified competition over cultural capital. Society became a stage on which the public face was fashioned as a model for emulation. Aestheticized culture had the effect of commodifying beauty, play and plea-sure, while the development of the money economy established a quantitative status hierarchy for the judgement and perception of beauty.

Self Help and Celebrity

The aestheticization of everyday life gradually accentuated ordinary culture as the pre-eminent arena for celebrity and weakened the real and symbolic power of the Court. From the strata of the non-titled and the wage labourer came many of the leading iconic figures of the age. Napoleon was the son of a Corsican *procureur* – roughly the equivalent of a provincial British solicitor. George Stephenson, the inventor of the railway engine, began working life as an engine fireman. Michael Faraday, the scientist, was the son of a blacksmith. Charles Dickens was the son of an insolvent debtor and famously worked in a blacking factory as a boy. The painter J.M.W. Turner was the son of a Covent Garden barber and wig-maker. Benjamin Franklin, a polymath and leading example of Enlightenment cosmopolitanism, Andrew Jackson and Abraham Lincoln, respectively the seventh and sixteenth Presidents of America, all achieved celebrity and influence from economically precarious, not to say indigent, beginnings. All were achieved celebrities, and their energy, talents and vigour in attaining prominence in public culture contrasted sharply with the trappings of ascribed celebrity. Not unreasonably, the stories of how these individuals ascended to wealth, esteem and influence were of considerable interest to the public.

Samuel Smiles, the ideologue and moralist *par excellence* of self-discipline and striving, published his enormously influential book on achieved celebrity, *Self Help*, in 1859. *Self Help* was an early example of a mid-Victorian popular therapy and counselling book. It mixed anecdotes and precepts selected from studying the lives of achieved celebrities in science, politics, commerce, industry and the arts, and portrayed them as holding lessons for those aspiring to upward mobility. The book was partly an attack on idleness and selfishness. It defended work as the handmaiden of self-discipline and moral probity. It was also a declaration of the superiority of possessive individualism over all other moral and social philosophies. It argued that national progress is nothing but the sum of individual enterprise, energy and uprightness. But above all it was an archive of achieved celebrity.

For Smiles, celebrity carried with it public responsibilities and duties. He disapproved of hedonistic or tyrannical celebrity, a phenomenon he dismissed as 'Caesarism', which he understood as 'human idolatry in its worst form – a worship of mere power, as degrading in its effects as the worship of mere wealth'.[6] Against this Smiles argued for Christian 'energetic individualism', a doctrine of self-improvement and progress that recognizes no limitation of birth or family background. Energetic individualism placed the onus of self improvement upon personal endeavour and acknowledged Christian respect and duties in relation to society. Smiles rejected the proposition that achieved celebrity should be thought of as an end in itself. Rather, the purpose of celebrity, whether in the achieved, ascribed or attributed form, is to add value to economy and culture and reinforce the Christian moral framework. Underlying this is a robust sense of the higher responsibilities of nationalism. Through the countless acts of individual self-improvement the progress of the nation is attained, and its leadership of the Empire solidified.

Self Help was not an attack on high culture. For example, Smiles recognized the validity of ascribed status hierarchies and the place of the aristocracy in society. In his conclusion he invoked the aristocratic model of 'the true gentleman' as the goal of self help. According to Smiles, the true gentleman is distinguished by the qualities of self-respect, generosity of spirit, honesty, uprightness and a keen sense of honour. While these qualities are often stereotypically associated with ascribed titular rank, Smiles insisted that the aristocracy possessed no monopoly over them. On the contrary, they proliferate in all walks of life. The vitality of working life produced new opportunities for upward mobility and for the poor to nurture gentlemanly qualities. *Self Help* acknowledged the virtues of aristocratic culture, but it identified the labouring masses as the main recruiting ground for the 'great apostles' of science, literature and art.

Self Help went through several editions and became known colloquially as 'the gospel of work'. It sold throughout the industrial world until well into the twentieth century, and made Smiles himself a celebrity. In as much as there is a consistent set of theoretical propositions in the book, it is that energetic individualism provides social order and prosperity, and achieved celebrity ennobles humankind by representing human perfection to the masses and providing a model for emulation. In *Leviathan* (1651), Thomas Hobbes gave political economy's classical account of how social order and prosperity is achieved. He argued that the state of nature is a war of all against all. Domination is not a satisfactory solution to this state of affairs, since it creates an obvious cleavage in society that inevitably ends in conflict. Hobbes propounded the view that the social contract, which recognized individual rights and limits natural freedom, is the correct solution to the war of all against all. Smiles's argument is a version of social contract theory. *Self Help* placed the responsibility for improvement squarely on the shoulders of the individual, and it recognized that labour was expended in the name of Christ.

Both Hobbes and Smiles are profoundly conservative thinkers. Each refrains from interrogating the specific, historical character of the economic and social principles that allocate honorific status and wealth, and still less from positing a more just and equal societal alternative. The discussion of achievement is conducted in the language of individualism. In Smiles, achieved celebrities are explicitly portrayed as role models. The intent was to encourage emulation. and by this means to reinforce a form of social order constructed around possessive individualism and market society. Smiles identified celebrity with utility. His lives of the famous concentrated on figures who added value to the economic and social fabric through invention, entrepreneurship, scholarship and artistic achievement.

Yet the enlargement of mass communications in the nineteenth century also expanded prurient interests. Books like Arthur Griffith's *The Chronicles of Newgate* (1883), drawing on *The Newgate Calendar*, which first appeared in the second half of the eighteenth century, discussed celebrity thieves, murderers, forgers, assassins, confidence men and highwaymen, and sanctimoniously recounted their last moments on the scaffold. The *succès de scandale* achieved by the sexual confessions in the anonymously authored *My Secret Life* (1888) pointed to a buoyant readership for whom moral and sexual transgression was a consuming interest. Celebrity culture could not be confined to respectable figures of emulation, as Smiles and others intended. In addition, social critics and individuals who were prepared to transgress moral and cultural boundaries became figures of cult interest. For in taking society itself, rather than the business of the Court, as the focus of interest, celebrity culture gradually reflected the personality types, social habits, adventurist impulses, hectic passions, moral and immoral desires, behavioural mutations, psychological urges and defences from which society is composed in all their prolific variety. The rise of celebrity culture did not reflect a growing fascination for the achievements of individual men and women. Rather, it underlined a grow-ing fascination with the *form* of society. In particular, the characteristic appearance, or habitus, of achievement, the pleasures and pains of instant recognition, the moral consequences of accumulated wealth, the variation of talents and the gullibility of the public all became richly explored themes in celebrity culture.

Staged Celebrity

James Boswell's *The Life of Samuel Johnson* (1791) was a landmark work in lionizing the life of a public figure who lived as an accessory of public culture and whose writings had done much to reveal the vanities and foibles of both ascribed and achieved celebrity. Others had written of achieved celebrity before Boswell. But seldom had the biography of an achieved celebrity been used so singlemindedly to not merely ennoble the subject, but elevate the author as a public figure in his own right. Boswell's Johnson was indubitably a figure formed through social contact, expanded by the opinions, obsessions and conduct of his time, and his cultural monumentality was achieved through his acquisition and rendition of wisdom concerning the affairs of men. The same is true of the image that

Boswell wishes to project of himself, of the biographer as celebrity, perhaps the first such intervention since the days of Callisthenes. By chronicling the life of Johnson in exacting and, one might add, undeniably self-serving detail, Boswell both declared Johnson's historic importance and valorized his own identification with the life. Boswell's *Life of Johnson* signalled both the democratization of fame and the birth of modern fandom. For it concentrated on the performance and projection of achieved celebrity on society, and presented the biographer and audience as spectators who will benefit through emulation. The rise of achieved celebrity culture signifies the democratization of power in society. Achieved celebrities, drawn from the mass and form of the people, reflect the declining lustre and power of ascribed celebrity.

Staged celebrity refers to the calculated technologies and strategies of performance and self projection designed to achieve a status of monumentality in public culture. In cases where these technologies and strategies are successful, the achieved celebrity may acquire enduring iconic significance. Because democracy assumes the formal equality of the electorate, it requires leaders to be larger than the common man, so as to achieve influence over public opinion. Political leaders, therefore, soon became adept in staging celebrity. The gruelling and pious insistence of American presidents to speak 'for the American people' may utilize spectacular skills of ventriloquism that disguise the voice of capital or sectarian political interests, but when it works it can create lasting figureheads. Lincoln's journey from a log cabin to the White House and his subsequent martyrdom 'for the Union' is a case in point. When the novelist, sometime politician and media celebrity Gore Vidal wrote his novel *Lincoln* (1984), he complained that he was forced to resort to fiction in order to tell the real story because most biographical treatments of the President failed to rise above sugary hagiography. In effect, Vidal argued that it was necessary to rescue Lincoln from the imaginary public edifice raised over many decades by spin doctors and zealots.

Lincoln was, in fact, a master of staged celebrity. His plainsman oratory wooed voters, and was propounded with devastating political calculation and adroitness. His conduct of the Civil War was always directed with an eye to posterity. The Gettysburg Address was not merely a magnificent dirge for the Civil War dead, but a baptismal oration on the rebirth of the nation in Lincoln's own image.

But Lincoln was not the first president to understand the importance of staged celebrity in achieving political power. Establishing iconic significance in a culture is a valuable political asset because it carries with it automatic recognition, presupposes cultural authority and radiates glamour. Andrew Jackson was the first president to develop the technology and strategy of staged celebrity as a wholescale political weapon. In many ways Jackson was a typical nineteenth-century adventurer. He was a foot soldier in the American War of Independence. He was captured and imprisoned by the British. He fought a duel and shot dead Charles Dickinson, a Nashville socialite who had alleged improprieties over a horse-racing bet. He was a white supremacist and compulsive land-grabber who waged war against the Creek nation, and whose presidency masterminded the forced eviction of Native Americans from their homelands. Jackson's victory over the British at the Battle of New Orleans in 1815 turned him into a national hero. Arguably, the victory was decisive in the American state-formation process. Jackson was credited with restoring national pride and confidence. His presidential campaign utilized this reputation to present him as more fearless and resolute than rival candidates. He grasped the importance of the media in self-presentation and projection in the formation of public opinion, and he fashioned *The Globe* newspaper as the central instrument in his propaganda machine. *The Globe* provided Jackson with a platform to establish complete control over the Democratic party and to present a public front of heroic popular unity to the country.

The basic social and political equipment that raised Lincoln as magical and immortal to the American people was planned and engineered under the presidency of Andrew Jackson. His was an administration that exploited and developed staged celebrity as a primary political tool. Since Jackson, nearly every presidential campaign has sought to use the press to enhance the celebrity value of the campaign hopeful.

The growth of celebrity culture presented new opportunities for celebrity endorsement. From the days of Warren Harding, who was President in 1921–3, presidents have sought to woo voters by courting movie entertainers. This climaxed under the presidency of John F. Kennedy. He regularly used his movie actor brother-in-law Peter Lawford to bring Frank Sinatra, Sammy Davis Jnr and Marilyn Monroe to the White House. Kennedy's affair with Monroe symbolized the incestuous relationship between the political and movie strands of celebrity culture.

Richard Nixon, who grew up in California at a time when many Hollywood stars, such as Charlie Chaplin, Humphrey Bogart and Edward G. Robinson, were openly on the Left, remained relatively indifferent to Hollywood endorsement. Nixon was the embodiment of the insecure little man who had been denied favour on account of his background and unglamorous appearance. During his tenure in office only a handful of movie celebrities, notably John Wayne, were welcomed in the White House. The situation changed radically when Ronald Reagan was in office. Reagan was, of course, a former Hollywood actor himself, and appreciated the publicity value of celebrity culture. His 1981 inauguration was organized as a two-and-a-half-hour Hollywood extravaganza. The cavalcade of stars was hosted by Efrem Zimbalist Jnr, with readings from great American literature by Charlton Heston. Commentary was supplied by Johnny Carson. The audience was serenaded by Donny Osmond's free interpretation of a Chuck Berry classic, renamed 'Go Ronnie Go', Ethel Merman's rendition of 'Everything's Coming Up Roses' and Sinatra himself, singing 'Nancy With the Laughing Face' to the new First Lady.

Bill Clinton was known as the first rock 'n' roll President, who used movie and Pop stars to enhance his image. The unsuccessful 2000 presidential campaign of Al Gore received financial backing and public support from Robert De Niro, Harrison Ford, Michael Douglas, Jack Nicholson, Kevin Costner, Tom Hanks, Nicolas Cage, Richard Dreyfus, James Garner, Herbie Hancock, Oliver Stone, Rob Reiner, David Geffen, Michael Eisner, Stephen Spielberg, Gwyneth Paltrow, Sharon Stone, Jeanne Tipplehorn, Sheryl Crowe and Barbra Streisand.

In the UK, party leaders have been slow to emulate American-style presentational tactics. Harold Wilson's attempts to bring glamour into Downing Street by authorizing awards for The Beatles and '60s show-biz personalities now look clumsy, unheartfelt and embarrassing. The post-war election campaigns up to the mid-1980s were comparatively low key. Margaret Thatcher was projected as an apocalyptic leader who broke the mould of the welfare state and revitalized British individualism. Arguably, this was a triumph of spin over substance, for under her leadership Britain was racked with widespread social unrest and an equivocal economic performance. None the less, it was unquestionably popular with the electorate, who returned Thatcher to power in three successive elections. Her use of celebrities to endorse her politics was relatively modest, although the disc jockey and comedian Kenny Everett did notoriously address a national Conservative campaign conference in 1983 with the imprecation to 'bomb Russia'.

John Major's prime ministership was a return to the low-key leadership of the Wilson, Heath and Callaghan era. But in the 1990s this was abandoned under New Labour. Tony Blair was projected as the focal point of the Labour campaign. Perhaps because Blair's wife is the daughter of the actor Anthony Booth, Blair is not shy of consorting with celebrities in public. Noel and Liam Gallagher and other 'Brit Pop' brahmins have supped at Downing Street. Meetings with the public, campaign rallies and media interviews are conducted in the presidential style of self-projection and the cultivation of Christian righteous individualism that no doubt Samuel Smiles himself would have applauded.

Photography and Staged Celebrity

One of the key elements in making staged celebrity prominent in society was the invention of photography. The public image is logically crucial in the elevation and dissemination of the public face. Because the photograph is so ubiquitous in contemporary culture, it is easy to forget that its invention is not even 200 years old. In 1839 Louis Daguerre first exhibited to the French Academy the photographic process that he and J. N. Niepce had recently developed. In England William Henry Fox Talbot had been attempting to capture images on light-sensitive paper. By 1835 he had succeeded with this process by using gallic acid to develop paper 'negatives' that were made translucent by waxing and used to make prints. The essentials for the photographic revolution of culture were in place.

By the mid-1840s daguerreotype galleries were founded in Paris, London and New York. The versatility of photography as a conduit of news was richly demonstrated by Roger Fenton's photographs of the Crimean War (1854–6) and Matthew Brady's of the American Civil War (1861–5). But in addition, photographic portraiture offered new opportunities for staging celebrity. Gaspard-Félix Tournachon, or Nadar as he was known after 1849, argued that his photographs enabled the spectator to apprehend the habits, ideas, character and very essence of his subjects. His portraits of distinguished contemporaries, such as Daumier, Monet, Millet, Corot, Doré, Guys and Baudelaire, established the nineteenth-century template for portraying celebrities to the public. Photography rapidly eclipsed portraits in miniature as offering the best likeness of a subject.

In 1849 James Polk was the first incumbent American President to be photographed. Yet it was Lincoln again who exploited the technology to imprint his own image of solemnity, concentration and grandeur on the American imagination. He deliberately used photography to establish his presence as the personification of the nation. 'President Lincoln', declared Nathaniel Hawthorne, 'is the essential representative of Yankees, and the veritable specimen, physically, of what the world seems determined to regard as our characteristic qualities'.[7] Similar claims had been made on behalf of Washington, Jefferson and Jackson, but by Lincoln's day photography's technical improvements and declining cost offered unprecedented opportunities for breaking with the past by presenting what was generally perceived to be a truer, more intimate likeness. In 1854 the *carte-de-visite*, which consisted of a miniature portrait and signature, was introduced by André Disderi in France. Lincoln partly attributed his election victory in 1861 to the *carte-de-visite* made of him for the campaign by Matthew Brady.

Disderi's camera took ten photographs on a single glass plate, thereby offering the public affordable, mass-produced photographic keepsakes. As early as the 1860s, *cartes* of distinguished celebrities such as Queen Victoria, Longfellow and Ulysses Grant were avidly collected by fans. Nadar was an early convert. He rapidly developed a lucrative sideline to his prestige portraiture business. The *cartes* craze lasted well into the twentieth century, by which time it had become so extensive that cards showing famous sportsmen and women, actors and actresses were included free in cigarette packets.

Cartes certainly increased the prominence of celebrity culture by making celebrities more accessible to the public through photographic images. By becoming universally visible, the forms and varieties of celebrity culture became more pronounced in popular culture. However, it would be a mistake to suppose that photography simply had an edifying and improving effect. The *carte-de-visite* photograph was suitable for the circulation of pornographic pictures. As early as 1850 a law was passed in France outlawing the exhibition of obscene photographs in public places and making possession of negatives punishable by a prison sentence. Once again one is struck by celebrity culture's fascination with the mutation, repression and transgression of social form. The individual men and women photographed in the pornographic *cartes* were always anonymous, but their illegal pictorial proliferation after 1850 is testimony to the strength of interest in the allure of illegal, underground and immoral cultures. The same processes that led reformers like Samuel Smiles to bend society into a rational, uplifting shape organized around achieved celebrity worked to make notorieties of figures from the marginal and repressed regions of culture.

Police mug-shots of violent criminals are an example of this process. The intention behind them was to improve the surveillance, monitoring and control of the population. But by publicizing the physical identity of notorious figures who lived outside the law they also glamourized and mythologized them. By the 1930s the gangster Al Capone had become the civic landmark of Chicago, fêted by actors, scriptwriters and media moguls, and was frequently cheered by the public when he appeared at sports stadiums, restaurants and other public places. What the crowds responded to was partly Capone's power. By the late 1920s he controlled prostitution, gambling and bootlegging in Chicago's South Side and threat-ened to encroach on rival gangland territory on the North Side. Capone's gang was woven into the fabric of everyday life for half the city's popula-tion. But fear was only part of the key to his celebrity. By supplying illegal liquor and drugs to the Depression-hit population, he acquired gratitude, respect and a sort of murky popularity. Capone was no Robin Hood, but he did supply the poor with narcotic pleasures that the state had taken away. So in a concrete way he was regarded as a positive force in the eyes of many in America. His celebrity may have been seriously flawed, but it contributed colour and zest to a population burdened by prohibition and economic hardship. The St Valentine's Day massacre in 1929 was Capone's unsuccessful attempt to assassinate George 'Bugsy' Moran, who controlled the North Side gang. Seven of Moran's henchmen were slaughtered and the killings made global news, further elevating Capone's celebrity as a man who was beyond the law. Capone was the inspiration for several Hollywood mob films in the 1930s and '40s, most notably *Little Caesar* (1930), *Scarface* (1932) and *The Gangster* (1947). In making Capone, Charley (Lucky)

Luciano, Frank Costello, Vito Genovese, Meyer Lansky, Bugsy Siegel, Joey Adonis, Dutch Schultz and other criminals visible, photography and film produced the means for not only identifying gangsters, but also romanticizing them as popular bandits.

Photography, then, furnished celebrity culture with powerful new ways of staging and extending celebrity. It introduced a new and expanding medium of representation that swiftly displaced printed text as the primary means of communicating celebrity. Photographs made fame instant and ubiquitous in ways that the printed word could not match. Oscar Wilde's tour of the United States in 1882, in which Wilde regaled American audiences with his lectures on the new Aesthetic Movement in London, was a sensational triumph. Arguably, its popularity owed less to the quality of Wilde's musings on the glory of Hellenic art and culture and the wisdom of Walter Pater and John Ruskin on beauty, and rather more to the staged photographs of him taken by Napoléon Sarony in New York. These extraordinary representations of the young aesthete presented Wilde as an exotic Adonis, and were used to advertise his lectures throughout the USA.

Similarly, the spectacular success of Ernest Hemingway in the late 1920s and '30s was partly due to the glamorous sequence of photographs taken of him by Helen Breaker in 1928. Her photographs made Hemingway look like a film star, and greatly increased the appeal of his fiction to book clubs, newspaper syndicates and Broadway and Hollywood. Another example is Harold Harma's suggestive photograph of Truman Capote on the dust-jacket of Capote's first novel, *Other Voices, Other Rooms* (1948). This displayed the fully clothed author reclining on a well-upholstered chair with his hand languidly resting on his nether regions, which caused as much media comment as his prose. A number of magazines and papers reprinted it alongside the reviews, and the publisher, Random House, used it in ads – *'This is Truman Capote'* – and produced blow-ups for shop display.

The persona of the author was doubtless always an object of fascination for readers. Nineteenth-century literary giants, such as Baudelaire, George Sand, Dickens, Walt Whitman, Tennyson and Longfellow, all sat for photographic portraits, and their publishers used them to publicize their works. But by the 1920s and '30s publishing companies were publicizing writers like F. Scott Fitzgerald, Hemingway and Evelyn Waugh as celebrity icons, whose appearance and style in personifying the *Zeitgeist* were of equivalent cultural significance to their fiction. Harold Harma's insinuating photograph of Capote therefore developed a fairly well-worn precedent. Present-day authors such as Will Self, Jay McInerney, Martin Amis, Jeanette Winterson, Salman Rushdie and Bret Easton Ellis have extended the cult of personality, so that their public image arguably has more public recognition than their work.

The Cultural Impresario

The photographs of Wilde and Hemingway were part of marketing campaigns organized respectively by the producer and tour manager Richard D'Oyly Carte and Scribner's editor Maxwell Perkins. Wilde and Hemingway did not simply appear before the public; rather their appearance was orchestrated and managed by agents who headed teams of publicists and marketing personnel. By the end of the nineteenth century, the appearance of celebrities, celetoids and celeactors on the public stage presupposed the calculation and labour of cultural impresarios. Invariably, staged celebrity was now professionally managed.

The roots of the cultural impresario stretch back to ancient times. The ex-Roman consul Iunius Brutus Pera should be regarded as the first readily identifiable example of one. In 264 BC, in a ceremony to honour his dead father, he presented the first gladiatorial games, in an ox-market. The gladiatorial games became the *pièce de résistance* of spectacle in Roman life.

Their success required planning, advertising and the development of specialized presentation skills. The function of the impresario is not merely to entertain, but to locate and stage acts, and to publicize them, so as to induce a craving in the public.

The tradition of strolling players and the fairs in Europe during the Middle Ages amplified the role of cultural impresario by introducing the role of the touring manager. But until the sixteenth century these traditions exploited and developed the spirit of carnival as the primary attraction for audiences. The concentration of play-forms in a general single staged event, rather than the charisma of particular celebrity players, drew the crowds. Not until the emergence of the actor-managers in the Elizabethan age could staged celebrity properly be said to focus on the elevation of common individuals as 'sights to see'.

I have, however, already noted that the history of the theatre in the sixteenth and seventeenth centuries was chequered. Royal licences to perform restricted the content and range of performance. Moreover, limitations of transport and communication prevented the sense of national and global co-presence from flourishing. Instantaneous, omnipresent celebrity had to wait for the revolutions in industry, communication and transport of the eighteenth century before making a bow in the public arena. David Garrick revived the actor-manager tradition and raised it to new heights in publicizing celebrity. But it was not until the 1840s that the modern cultural impresario was properly born.

This development is probably connected to the crystallization of the organized institutions of modern urban society. Specifically, the national, formal organization of schools, factories, businesses, hospitals and government agencies into recognizably modern, rational–legal, bureaucratic forms can be traced to this time. With the growth of concentrated, fixed urban–industrial populations, commercial amusements began to be stripped of their connotations with peripatetic, desultory attractions and transformed into fixed, systematic programmes of entertainment, in which celebrities played the starring role.

The most important cultural impresario of the era was Phineas Taylor Barnum. Barnum realized that the fascination with social form lay at the heart of popular culture. By staging individuals as examples of exotic social form, Barnum recognized that he could make celebrities out of virtually nothing. The trick lay largely in the daring and presentational skills of the cultural impresario. Thus, in 1835 he began to exhibit Joice Heth, who purported to be a 161-year-old slave who had tended to George Washington. The success of the hoax opened Barnum's eyes to the economic potential of staging celebrity.

In 1841 he took over Scudder's failing American Museum on Broadway, with its ill-lit and poorly exhibited collection of sea-shells, minerals, stuffed birds and fossils, and relaunched it as 'Barnum's American Museum'. A lighthouse, 'Drummond Lamp', was installed on the roof of the building which cast a powerful reflector beam up and down Broadway by night, bathing the whole area in illustrious light. Barnum transformed the exterior by installing scores of paintings between all of the nearly one hundred windows on the upper stories. Now, from the front of the museum the public was confronted with enticing images of polar bears, elephants, lions, eagles, tapirs, giraffes, kangaroos and eagles. The effect was to transform the building into a 'dreamlike emporium'. Barnum added an ever-changing bill of live acts to the exhibits, such as Benjamin Pelham, 'the great Paganini whistler'; Yan Zoo, the Chinese juggler; and J. Nathans, the serpent charmer. Barnum organized aggressive advertising campaigns to publicize the Museum, and by 1850 it was New York's premier attraction.

The American Museum was intended to educate as well as entertain. From the earliest days Barnum was concerned to display anthropological exhibits that demonstrated the enormous variety and diversity of the human species. The 1860 catalogue and guidebook lists thirteen 'human curiosities' which were exhibited as a quasi-anthropology of humanity. They included an albino family (the Lucasies), The Living Aztecs (Maximo and Bartola, a brother and sister suffering from microcephaly), three dwarfs, a black mother with two albino children, The Swiss Bearded Lady, The Highland Fat Boys and What is It? (or more accurately, Harry Johnson, a mentally retarded man with microcephaly). Exhibiting the 'curiosities' was in questionable taste. But it showed more cogently than anything else the wisdom of Barnum's belief that mere social form could be staged as celebrity and that the public would accept it as such.

Barnum regarded the American Museum and his later travelling circus as his principal achievements. However, his fame as the outstanding cultural impresario of the nineteenth century rests primarily on his staging of Charles Sherwood Stratton, or 'General Tom Thumb', as Barnum christened him, and Jenny Lind, 'The Swedish Nightingale', as peerless celebrities of the age. Tom Thumb was wholly Barnum's invention. Barnum discovered the 25-inch boy, weighing fifteen pounds, by chance in Bridgeport, Connecticut. He coached him to imitate well-known mythical and historical individuals, including Cupid, Samson, Hercules, Robinson Crusoe, Cain, Romulus, Frederick the Great and Napoleon, and to perform a variety of tricks. Tom Thumb captivated New York, and later America and Europe. As Stratton aged he grew corpulent and his miniature appearance became less congenial to the public. However, when Barnum staged Tom Thumb's marriage to the 32-inch tall Lavinia Warren in 1863, it revived Tom's career and added Lavinia to Barnum's stable of attractions. Jenny Lind was already a celebrity in Europe when Barnum offered her the unprecedented sum of $150,000 to perform 150 concerts in America. Lind's soprano voice was rumoured to be angelic, but she was also revered as the embodiment of feminine artlessness, charity, innocence and piety. Barnum's publicity campaign for her tour began six months before her arrival in New York. He goaded the press to run approving reviews of her performances in Europe and organized the 'Jenny Lind Prize Song Contest', which promised a $200 award to the winning ode, which would be set to music and sung by Lind at her opening recital. A crowd of 20,000 welcomed her arrival. Among them, in an effort to maximize the hysteria, Barnum planted his own employees dressed in black suits and bearing bunches of red roses. Although Lind cut short her tour in 1851 after performing only 95 concerts, Barnum still grossed a revenue of $712,000 in less than a year.

Incidentally, Mathew Brady's 'Daguerrean Miniature Gallery' was located opposite 'Barnum's American Museum' on Broadway. Barnum, who possessed a remarkably keen understanding of the value of public relations and was never wary of using the latest technology to enhance his attractions, employed Brady to photograph Tom Thumb, Jenny Lind, the Lucasies, Eng and Chang, the Siamese Twins and Tom Thumb's wedding. Brady was also responsible for Barnum's *carte-de-visite*, and the *cartes* of Tom Thumb and Lavinia Warren.

The rise in power of the cultural impresario did not necessarily produce a relationship of dependence. Jenny Lind took it upon herself to cancel her American tour after performing only two thirds of her contracted concert dates, and Barnum was powerless to stop her. Not all celebrities have been so fortunate. In the field of popular music, Elvis Presley is now widely held to have been ruthlessly exploited by his manager, Colonel Tom Parker. Parker appropriated a large slice of royalties from Presley's recordings, performances and merchandise. He was also the architect of the misguided plan to turn Presley into a general entertainer in the early 1960s, by urging him to branch out into mainstream movies of negligible artistic merit.

Until his premature death in 1967, The Beatles were managed by Brian Epstein. Epstein's managerial touch on the group was notably lighter than Parker's on Presley. None the less, after discovering the group in the Cavern Club, Liverpool in 1961, Epstein ran all of the band's financial, touring and public relations. The early construction of its public face was largely Epstein's brainchild. For example, it was at Epstein's instigation that the band wore suits on stage for the first time in 1962. After the band decided to cease touring in 1966, Epstein's influence diminished. Despite this, after his death, the band experienced major difficulties in public impression management. Confessions of drug use by Lennon and McCartney were greeted with consternation by many fans, and the *Magical Mystery Tour* (1968) TV special was regarded as incomprehensible by critics and many fans alike. By 1969 the haemorrhage of funds from Apple, the mass-media company founded by the band, prompted Lennon to claim that they were staring personal bankruptcy in the face. The solution, devised by Lennon, Harrison and Ringo Starr, was to introduce the American music entrepreneur Allen Klein to manage them. McCartney rejected Klein, and the resulting rift with the other members of the band ultimately led to the break-up of The Beatles.

One of the major influences on Pop, fashion and youth culture in the 1970s and '80s was David Bowie. Bowie was noted for his chameleon-like propensity to change image and style regularly. Between 1966 and 1970 he was managed by Ken Pitt, who initially seemed intent on turning Bowie from a mod into a cabaret singer in the manner of Anthony Newley, and encouraged him to produce the embarrassing novelty single 'The Laughing Gnome'. Under Pitt, Bowie developed into a progressive folk-rock singer and achieved his first major hit with 'Space Oddity', which reached number five in the UK chart. But his album failed to make an impression, and Bowie broke with Pitt and contracted to a new manager, Tony Defries.

The poor sales of his first album release under Defries's management, a progressive rock album, *The Man Who Sold the World* (1971), threatened to cast Bowie in the unenviable role of a one-hit wonder. However, Defries seized on Bowie's interest in experimentation and absorption with popular culture. Bowie compared himself to a Xerox machine that photocopied Pop influences and produced a composite that was culturally unique. Defries decided to make this capacity to express ambiguity and change the centrepiece of his marketing strategy. The cover of *The Man Who Sold the World* pictured Bowie wearing a dress, and Defries exploited the growing public interest in the limits of hetero-normativity by presenting Bowie as the first bisexual rock star. *Hunky Dory* (1971) continued the image of sexual ambiguity with a cover that feminized Bowie's appearance and tracks that celebrated fatherhood with the same apparently sincere enthusiasm as gay cruising. *Hunky Dory* was a commercial success and increased Bowie's profile as a high-potential recording artist. However, it was the invention of 'Ziggy Stardust' that made Bowie a global phenomenon. Ziggy Stardust was a character with an androgynous, flamboyantly outrageous appearance that Bowie described as 'a cross between Nijinsky and Woolworth's'. The traditional rock idol of the 1960s was a sexually coherent figure of rebellion: Mick Jagger, Jimi Hendrix, Jim Morrison. The appeal of Ziggy Stardust lay partly in the incoherence of the public face. By mixing style, femininity, masculinity and camp in one character, Bowie created a face that did not urge public emulation, but enabled the public to escape from the humdrum of their sexual, work and family commitments. *The Rise and Fall of Ziggy Stardust* (1972) and the accompanying tours elevated Bowie into the top flight of global rock stars. It was followed by *Aladdin Sane* (1973) and *Diamond Dogs* (1974), both of which were huge commercial successes.

But by 1975 Bowie was at odds with Defries and his company, Mainman. Bowie avowed that he had 'slaved for nothing' since 1970. The legal termination of their contract is generally judged to have been very favourable to Defries. Mainman was paid 50 per cent of Bowie's royalties from *Hunky Dory* to *David Live*, and a further 16 per cent of all gross earnings, from all sources, until September 1982. After the meeting Bowie allegedly returned to his New York apartment and howled for a week.

The rise of Punk in the mid-1970s produced new opportunities for cultural impression management. Punk was the antithesis of the mellow, non-violent values of the hippies, the *nouveau riche* self-regard of successful '60s performers and the Grand Guignol of the '70s Glitter generation. In its purest expression, Punk articulated the frustrations of working-class youth who would never get to Woodstock or escape the drudgery of high-density housing and low wages. It articulated rage and pent-up violence. But Punk was also a commercial exercise. Arguably, the central Punk band was The Sex Pistols. The cultural impresario behind them was Malcolm McLaren, who previously had briefly managed The New York Dolls and owned the Sex boutique selling bondage gear in London's King's Road. McLaren was a devotee of French Situationism. He appreciated the privileged role that spectacle plays in Pop culture and savoured the old Situationist slogan that 'boredom is counter-revolutionary'. He recruited the members of the band from his boutique, which was renamed Seditionaries in 1977, supplied them with an outrageous name, provided them with rehearsal space and instilled in them the publicity value of confrontation and spontaneity. McLaren's approach was to openly question the validity of established criteria of cultural and counter cultural cachet. In particular, he lambasted the millionaire rock groups and solo performers of the 1960s and early '70s for turning into complacent, self-satisfied overlords of popular culture. The Sex Pistols were designed to articulate the word from the streets. Their poor musicianship and confrontational style merely served to enhance the impression of honesty and integrity.

When The Sex Pistols acrimoniously broke up, McLaren contrived to persuade the media that the band had always been a con and a vehicle for financial accumulation. This was designed to highlight his own role as a cultural impresario who had successfully hoodwinked the mass-media and the fans. McLaren maintained that Pop music was of no value, and success was a matter of manipulating the media and the public. Julian Temple's film *The Great Rock 'n' Roll Swindle* (1979), orchestrated by McLaren, is a full-length, populist presentation of this case. It was no more than a partial success. If The Sex Pistols were designed as a con, several of their recordings, notably 'Anarchy in the UK', 'God Save the Queen' and 'Pretty Vacant', captured the sense that rock, by the early 1970s, had fallen into ineffable self-parody. Punk articulated the new frustrations of post-war baby-boomers who found that the declining rate of economic growth meant they could not get the jobs their education had prepared them for.

The Corporatized Impresario

The cultural impresario is a cultural intermediary who manages the chains of attraction between a performer and an audience for a profit. Cultural impresarios present celebrities in sensationalized terms so as to maximize their attraction. Celetoids are an accessory of this culture. Cultural impresarios are central in moulding the public face of celetoids and presenting them as objects of intense, evanescent public preoccupation. In contrast, celebrities represent a more durable form of attraction over the public. As the twentieth century developed, the conduct of their careers tended to take the form of corporate, rather than personal, management.

Consider the Hollywood studio system. It had its roots in the silent film days. But it was overhauled and refined during the 1930s and '40s by movie moguls such as Irving Thalberg, Louis B. Mayer, David Selznick, Samuel Goldwyn and Jack Warner. The UK developed a weaker version of the system under studio czars that included Sir Alexander Korda and J. Arthur Rank. The Hollywood system treated the studio as a business corporation and stacked enormous powers in the hands of producers. They were able to hire out contract players to other studios for a fee, block or rewrite scripts, and veto projects selected by stars who were under contract to them. Thalberg, in particular, acquired the reputation for ruthless firmness and iron business judgement. F. Scott Fitzgerald based the mogul in his novel *The Last Tycoon* (1941) on him. The producer regarded his main loyalty as to the corporation. Where necessary he subordinated the interests of the celebrities under his control for the corporation's benefit. The cultural impresario representing the celebrity was no longer able to determine all elements of the presentation of the public face of the celebrity.

Already, by the 1930s, the sheer scale and cost of movie production required the form of the corporation to produce, market and distribute the product. The role of cultural impresarios began to change subtly. They moved from being all-purpose showmen, *à la* Barnum, to being business agents who represented their clients' interests by contracting them to a studio, leasing them to a rival studio for specific projects or managing specialized public relations exercises, in a word selling them like a *commodity*. The relationship between the agent and the studio producer became pivotal in developing celebrity careers. The studio system lasted until the mid-1960s, and is generally regarded to have been, on balance, a stifling influence on artistic freedom.

The studio system was successfully challenged in the late 1960s by the rise of independent film-makers. However, after a relatively short interregnum that lasted until the mid-1970s, the revolution of independent films petered out. A new intrusive system of control, the axial principle of which was the relationship between the agent and the corporation, became ascendant. Cultural impresarios like the egregious Don Simpson, who produced *Flashdance* (1983), *Beverly Hills Cop 1* and *2* (1984, 1987), *Top Gun* (1986), *Days of Thunder* (1990), *Crimson Tide* (1995), *Dangerous Minds* (1995) and *The Rock* (1996), became dominant in determining the narrative, casting, style and even the soundtrack of a film. But they did so in liaison with studios who were ultimately answerable to parent corporations like Disney, Seagram (owners of Universal), Time Warner and Sony.

Simpson is widely credited with inventing the 'high concept' in movie production. Others claim that it was invented by either Barry Diller during his term as programming executive at ABC in the early '70s, or Michael Eisner, currently head of Disney films, during his period at Paramount. *High concept* refers to the stripping down of narrative content to a sole, simple idea that will be immediately grasped by audiences in order to galvanize their interest. The script-writer Chip Proser, who was involved in development work for *Top Gun*, recalled that Simpson's original high-concept pitch was simplicity itself. 'It was two guys in leather jackets and sunglasses standing in front of the biggest, fastest, fucking airplane you ever saw in your life'.[8] The eventual plot of the movie is remarkably faithful to this idea. A stereotypal collection of rival trainee fighter pilots compete, for several weeks of intense aerial combat, to win the coveted 'Top Gun trophy', which provides the winner with the plum job of a Top Gun flight instructor. The one-dimensional characters are part of a tapestry in which velocity and hazard really have the starring roles. Indeed, high concept presupposes minimal character development, so as to maximize the physical aspects of the characters, notably their appearance and demeanour. Music is a short cut to establishing presence, motive and style. For example, in Paul Schrader's *American Gigolo* (1980), the Giorgio Moroder /Blondie song 'Call Me' is used to illustrate the daily routine of the high-priced gigolo Julian Kay (Richard Gere). The song is used as the backdrop to Julian buying expensive clothes, preening and driving in his Mercedes to meet female clients.

Simpson understood the value of product placement, and constructed his high-concept movies around a soundtrack that included a potential hit. For example, Glenn Frey's 'The Heat is On' was the hit song from the soundtrack of *Beverly Hills Cop*; Irene Cara's 'What a Feeling' was the hit for *Flashdance*; and the Giorgio Moroder/Tom Whitlock song 'Take My Breath Away' was a number one hit from *Top Gun*. Simpson both anticipated, and was influenced by, the production values of the promotional Pop video and MTV.

Network television has adopted the high concept strategy in the development of quiz shows like *Blind Date, Who Wants to be a Millionaire?* and *The Other Half. Who Wants to be a Millionaire?* was developed in Britain. It has been exported worldwide and is generally regarded to be one of the most successful quiz formats of the turn of the century. The entire show revolves around the simple principle that contestants answer a series of questions that might lead to them winning £1 million. Each round of questions becomes progressively harder and contestants have the option to ask the studio audience and phone a friend if they are stuck. But these options are fixed, and once they are exhausted, contestants are on their own.

High concept is the apotheosis of the cultural impresario's art. It reduces aesthetic and narrative content to the lowest economic denominator of the marketplace. The ramifications of a single sensational idea are worked out obsessively, but without any interest in commenting on, or reforming, culture or society. High concept might be defined as mass entertainment without reflection.

For example, *Armageddon*, produced by Don Simpson's old partner, Jerry Bruckheimer, was the number one box office film of 1998, grossing $202 million. The plot is pure high concept. A giant meteor is being sucked into the earth's orbit, and collision will mean the end of the world. Around this simple, but arresting notion is embroidered a story of Harry Stamper (Bruce Willis), a maverick explosives expert working in the oil-drilling business. Somewhat implausibly, Stamper and his team are identified as the only munitions experts capable of destroying the meteor. NASA trains them and puts them into outer space, where, after some staged mishaps, Stamper detonates the meteor and saves the world, albeit by sacrificing himself in the process.

What is interesting about *Armageddon* and high-concept movies in general is their inherent conservatism. The film opens by lampooning Greenpeace, whose members are staging a protest against Stamper's oil rig. Stamper is a classic Hollywood example of the rugged individualist, one who is only summoned to save the world when government has palpably failed. The rockets that send him and his crew to intercept the meteor are called 'Freedom' and 'Independence'. The subplot between Stamper and his earthbound daughter, played by Liv Tyler, reinforces traditional family values. Stamper's martyrdom draws his daughter closer to his wayward surrogate son, played by Ben Affleck, who is a young rugged individualist in Stamper's mould, and makes their marriage inevitable.

There was bound to be a reaction against the corporatization of Hollywood. *Prima facie*, the success of the *Blair Witch Project* (1999), which returned a huge profit on a small investment, seemed to signal the return to the heyday of the independents. But the difference between 2001 and the 1960s is that the corporations and their studio affiliates are not in crisis. There is no real sense that corporations have lost touch with popular taste or that they are bankrolling films which, aesthetically and politically, belong to another era. What the independents have done is to point to gaps in the consumer market that Hollywood had not spotted.

Hollywood corporations have responded to the challenge by absorbing independents. Disney now owns Miramax, Seagram owns October and Time Warner owns New Line Cinema. Film commentators refer to the rise of 'Indiewood', in which the creative, risk-taking values of independent film makers are supported by the wealth and 'guidance' of the parent corporation. This is probably not going to be a marriage made in heaven. The commercial logic of the corporation requires executives to produce a profit in the long run. The independent film-maker is impelled to follow a quite contrary logic, one driven by aesthetic considerations. In cases where there is an irreconcilable division between business and aesthetic logic, the tendency is for business logic to triumph. Thus, the aesthetic values developed in Indiewood are likely to be subordinated to the dictate of the corporate balance sheet. The power that corporations now exercise over film distribution and marketing mean that if independent film-makers break from the corporation and try to flourish autonomously, their films are likely to be confined to the margins of popular culture.

CHAPTER FOUR

Celebrity and Transgression

In June 2000 in London, David Copeland, a 24-year-old engineer, was sentenced to six life terms following a bombing campaign that killed three persons and injured 139 others. Copeland, dubbed 'the Soho nail bomber' by the press, was found guilty of planting three nail bombs, the last one killing three people, one of whom was a pregnant woman, and injuring and maiming dozens, as well as terrorizing thousands of Londoners in April 1999. Two of the bombs targeted black and Asian communities in Brixton and Brick Lane. In the third, most devastating, incident the *Admiral Duncan* pub in the heart of Soho's gay district was bombed.

A notable feature of Copeland's arrest and trial was his evident enthusiasm at being caught and the prospect of elevation before the public via the mass-media. Police described his mood upon arrest as 'exhilarated'. He confessed immediately. He said that he longed to be captured so as to become famous. 'I've been dreaming about this for ages', he told police. 'Doing what I did, getting caught, going to court – it's my destiny. If no one remembers who you were, you never existed.' Throughout interrogation he was helpful in giving the full facts of how he made and planted the three explosive devices. He approached captivity not as a challenge to dissemble his veridical self, but as a stage to parade it before the world. He was jubilant about the prospect of the trial and complained that he felt 'cheated' when other groups claimed responsibility for the bombings.

Every murder, like every suicide, is partly an enigma. Outwardly, the motivation may seem straightforward, but the concatenation of factors that compel someone to take the life of others, or to end one's own life, is highly complex. Press coverage of the Copeland trial seized on his alleged homophobia and racism. It emerged that Copeland had been a member of the right-wing National Socialist Movement. Police discovered two Nazi flags and a photo collage of bomb incidents and blast victims when they searched his home. During interrogation Copeland was unapologetic about his hatred for ethnic minorities and gays. He showed no remorse for his male victims, but expressed regret at the death of the pregnant woman in the *Admiral Duncan* explosion. One Home Office psychiatric report suggested that his homophobia disguised repressed homosexuality. Be that as it may, there is ample evidence to suggest the view that Copeland was indeed a white supremacist and homophobe.

It is perhaps short-sighted to stop there, because this defines Copeland *a priori* as a psychopath and sociopath. As a result, medical diagnosis is privileged over cultural and sociological investigation in the analysis of his conduct. Rather like the 'lone nut' theory used to explain the assassinations of John F. Kennedy and Martin Luther King, Copeland is categorized as an isolated misfit who allowed his morbid delusions about race and sexuality to get the better of him. As such, he is translated into the category of a freak or aberration that is metaphysically divorced from the rules of the world at large. He is rendered as a folk demon belonging to a different race of humankind. His behaviour is thus pathologized, and the relation of ordinary life to his behaviour is minimized.

Murderers are not aliens. On the contrary, if one takes the Post-structuralist/Postmodern view that the human psyche is fragmented and mobile, it follows that, in certain circumstances, a reconfiguration of fragments stimulated by external circumstance might lead anyone to kill. Equally, the ease with which serial killers such as Ted Bundy, John Wayne Gacy, Ian Brady and Myra Hindley, Peter Sutcliffe (the 'Yorkshire Ripper') and Fred and Rosemary West resumed ordinary social interaction after murder suggests that killing does not outwardly identify one as psychologically abnormal. Therefore, tabloid polarization between 'ordinary', 'decent' people and murdering 'monsters' is unhelpful.

Certainly, Copeland did not regard himself to be an aberration. He believed he was in better contact with his veridical self than others, and resolved to express it irrespective of the consequences. As he wrote in a letter published in *The Mirror* newspaper: 'I am no monster, but some kind of terrorist, someone who puts themselves forward for what they believe in.' Copeland's actions suggest the self-image of the anti-hero, in as much as he did not flinch from following through the logic of his convictions. In cultivating and applying them Copeland saw himself to be more consistent and truthful than most 'ordinary' people.

Police interrogation revealed that his political and religious thinking was half-baked. He idolized ill-assorted Fascist leaders like Hitler and Saddam Hussein, and bracketed them with Stalin and the American serial killer Henry Lee. There was no coherent political analysis or strategy of transformation in his point of view. The evidence suggests that Copeland's real preoccupation lay not so much with politics *per se*, as with extremism. Notorious figures who acquire fame through inhuman acts thronged his fantasies. He regarded himself to be an alert and truthful man adrift in a society of sleepwalkers and hypocrites, and he wanted what ordinary people were generally too timid and reserved to grasp for themselves: fame.

We have an unusually detailed picture of Copeland's preoccupation with celebrity because *The Mirror* newspaper published extensive extracts of private letters he wrote while awaiting trial. The letters were written to a correspondent that Copeland believed to be a female penfriend. Actually, the correspondent was a male hoaxer who made the letters available to *The Mirror*. Written over a six-month period, Copeland's letters reveal a morbid interest in his own celebrity. He repeatedly inquires whether websites carry news or comments about him. He fantasizes that he and his correspondent could have been a modern-day Bonnie and Clyde. He writes approvingly when his photograph is printed on the front page of newspapers. His letters are concerned to establish his singularity and integrity and to confirm his celebrity status in the sight of the British public. 'So many people live such boring lives', he writes, 'getting up for work every day – dying with no one to miss them. That's not the life for me.'

Violence and the Celebrity Race

In as much as the celebrity race is ubiquitous, it is perhaps relevant to analyse part of Copeland's motive as an attempt to acquire fame. The normal pattern of achieved celebrity involves public acclaim and the ritualization of bonds of recognition and belonging. If the desire to 'be someone' is not achieved by 'normal' means, some individuals will have a compelling propensity to use violence as a means of acquiring fame through notoriety. The use of violence may be interpreted as an act of revenge on society for not recognizing the extraordinary qualities of the individual. After all, democratic culture encourages us to think that all are important, and all are special. Where the course of life does not fulfil these expectations, an individual may experience powerful feelings of frustration, rejection and invalidation. These feelings may be transferred onto society or onto a 'celestial' representative of society, namely a celebrity. Hence, perhaps the celebrity race is one factor in exploring the aetiology of so-called 'meaningless, high-profile crime' and stalking. Needless to say, incidents of terrorism, murder and serial killing cannot be interpreted as the reflection of feelings of frustration at failing to win public acclaim in the celebrity race. In every case, the reasons behind these actions require empirical investigation. Invariably this reveals violent conduct to be the result of a complex interplay of psychological factors involving the family, sexuality, politics, work and the other relevant institutions of social life. The argument I am making here is that the celebrity race should be recognized as one institution in social life that may prove to be relevant as a factor in precipitating some forms of violent behaviour. Copeland's bombing campaign cannot simply be regarded as a quest for acclaim, since it led to him being demonized by press and public alike. On the other hand, given his own published account, it is reasonable to interpret his conduct as a quest for recognition, a strategy for being accepted as special and extraordinary. To some extent, the dynamics of modern society mean that all of us are caught up in the celebrity race. It is axiomatic that only a minority acquire the public acclaim and recognition that we associate with celebrity status. It is also axiomatic that if the majority suffer from feelings of rejection and invalidation, they internalize them in ways that pose no threat to the social order. The proposition I wish to explore in this chapter is that some individuals transfer feelings of rejection and invalidation onto celebrities, who are regarded as representatives of social recognition and belonging, or externalize these feelings onto society at large for failing to recognize their special qualities.

Freud held that creative artists are chiefly motivated by the desire to achieve fame, wealth and sexual fulfilment. Generally speaking, celebrities are richer than ordinary people, possess greater opportunities for sexual liaisons with attractive partners, have more power to evade the intrusions of the law, and, for the most part, move about more easily in society. This is certainly the public perception, and it is one reason why celebrity status is so widely coveted and fantasized about. To some degree the desire for celebrity is a refutation of social convention. Transgression, one might postulate, is intrinsic to celebrity, since to be a celebrity is to live outside conventional, ordinary life.

Every accountant will tell you there is no gain without pain. In the midst of their wealth, political access and sexual possibilities, celebrities doubtless reflect on the burdens attendant upon celebrity status. Being stalked by the *paparazzi*, pestered by autograph-hunters and taunted by strangers figure prominently in the litany of complaints made by celebrities in respect of their fame. The incidence of marital tension, divorce and family discord are higher among the celebritariat than the average. The same goes for rates of mental illness and mortality. Elevation clearly intensifies what Georg Simmel called the 'radioactivity' of the individual, and this has personal costs as well as benefits. But given the ratio between winners and losers in the celebrity race, and the enormous material gains and status boost for winners, perhaps the whys and wherefores of celebrity status do not keep Britney Spears or Will Smith awake at night. What does keep some of their fans awake at night are fantasies about the lives that these people are leading, the wealth that surrounds them, the automatic popularity they enjoy, the doors that are open to them. The appetite for celebrity reflects a satiated thirst for the responsibilities and rules that pin down the rest of us.

Without doubt, celebrity is a widely desired characteristic of modern life, but the chances of gaining it via achieved celebrity are limited. Although it is relevant to comment on how celebrities themselves deal with the opportunities for transgression that celebrity status permits, this can be postponed here. The immediate question is to examine the relationship between transgression and the desire to achieve celebrity status in ordinary, everyday culture.

Achievement Famine and its Consequences

Most ordinary people suffer from *achievement famine*, a psychological condition that results from frustrated desires for material and romantic achievement of the sort the rich and famous enjoy. The democratic ideal of being recognized as extraordinary, special or unique collides with the bureaucratic tendency to standardize and routinize existence. Of course, it does not follow that achievement famine is necessarily the cause either of low self-esteem or violent reaction, although Robert Merton's analysis of 'criminality and the American Dream' (part of his attack on material inequality in American society) is remindful of the fact that in cases where desire strongly exceeds legitimate opportunity, there is a propensity for individuals to use illegitimate means to achieve the realization of their desires.[1] Even so, most of us, most of the time, gain renown and honorific status through unsung relations with our family, workmates and friends.

Paradoxically, it should be noted in passing that the celebrities who are the target of fan wish fulfilment are themselves frequently the victims of achievement fatigue or achievement mirage. *Achievement fatigue* is the psychological condition in which the individual who has attained a desired public face, and the recognition that accompanies it, experiences acclaim as a burden or sequence of diminishing returns. *Achievement mirage* refers to the recognition that achieved celebrity is shallow and false. 'I never wanted this in the first place', complained Kurt Cobain when he became an object of mass adulation and media intrusion in the early 1990s. Cobain's suicide was widely interpreted as a product of his alienation from celebrity culture. It was an extreme case of achievement mirage. However, it is not uncommon for celebrities to attempt to walk away from fame. Greta Garbo, Doris Day, Lon Chaney, Daniel Day Lewis and Howard Hughes voluntarily withdrew from the celebrity limelight, invariably in a bid to defend or regain the veridical self. John Lennon famously decided to stop recording after the birth of his second son in order to spend time with his family and relieve himself of the trappings of celebrity status.

Acquisitive society enjoins individuals to compete for wealth and status achievement, since these are the universal marks of distinction in the social order. Achievement famine is the psychological corollary of the acquisitive society. The profusion of celetoids and celeactors may be distracting us from this psychological condition by providing an achievement plague in which trivial or mundane incidents project individuals into celebrity culture. In a society in which the pseudo-event can catapult the media into a frenzy of reportage and cod punditry, the range of celetoids who pass before the public eye, for whatever reason, necessarily appears to be eclectic and ever-changing. Andy Warhol's famous remark – anyone can be famous for fifteen minutes – was Warhol relishing the inexorable rise of the pseudo-event and the celetoid.

Inasmuch as this is the case, celetoids and celeactors may be interpreted as revealing a profound sense of loss or absence in popular culture. In part, the decline of organized religion and community is the cause of this sense of loss. As Weberian sociology speculates, religious belief can operate as the remedy to achievement famine by promising righteous salvation in the life to come. With the decline of organized religion, deep romantic love and material success become the hallmarks of achievement. The fact that these are obviously very unevenly spread in society reinforces the proposition that achievement famine is the general psychological condition in contemporary culture.

It may seem a big leap to move from the recognition of achievement famine as a general symptom of the acquisitive society to the proposition that the quest for achieved celebrity is a demonstrable motive in many acts of homicide. Yet the proposition is quite uncontroversial in the criminological literature on murder. Jack Katz's superb phenomenology of crime is a case in point.[2] He begins by criticizing the orthodox link between deprivation and criminality. Generations of criminologists and social theorists have followed Robert Merton in interpreting violent crime as a response to an unsatisfactory family background or low socio-economic status. Katz criticizes this for failing to consider criminality in the criminal's own terms. It is unsatisfactory to attribute acquisition as a dominant motive in crime, for stolen goods are often discarded or destroyed. The desire to break rules is often evident in early adolescence, before acquisitive aspirations have been internalized. Criminals are frequently driven by the overwhelming compulsion to be different, to possess fame, to break boundaries, 'to be a star – something literally, distinctively transcendent'. This argument seeks to strip criminality of connotations with guilt and deprivation and to restore to it the denotations of excitement, pleasure and daring associated with the celebrity race. Criminality is, in part, the expression of the quest for one-upmanship, the desire to outsmart others and take people for a ride so as to confirm one's inner sense of superior gamesmanship. The argument does not dismiss the long-standing correlation between low socio-economic status and acquisitive crime. However, it submits that the meaning of deviance must be studied by reference to the *quality* of the concrete deviant act, rather than by dint of quantitative cross-matching with socio-economic data.

Seen from this perspective, many criminal acts become more intelligible. For example, consider the famous 1920s Leopold and Loeb murder case, in which two prosperous and outwardly respectable University of Chicago alumni, both with good grades and excellent career prospects, set out to commit the perfect crime. They murdered a 14-year-old boy, Bobby Franks, concealed the body in swampland, and demanded a ransom. The crime is generally remembered as a classic *folie à deux*. Leopold and Loeb were self-regarding homosexual lovers who, independently, would probably never have murdered. Each possessed individual personality traits which, when combined, produced an irresistible impulse to murder. Neither needed the money. Their purpose was calculated brinkmanship, designed to outwit the police and legal authorities in order to test their sub-Nietzschean theory that the 'Superman' lives beyond ordinary moral considerations. Their desire for public acclaim was peculiarly introverted, since it depended on the public failing to recognize them as the crime's perpetrators. One might postulate an inverted form of celebrity motivation here, in which public anonymity is a source of gratification and the reinforcement of celestial status. (Incidentally, the British serial killer Dr Harold Shipman also seems to have gained gratification and a sense of reinforced superiority by outwitting the authorities.) During their trial Leopold and Loeb were obsessively concerned to establish a self-regarding sense of intellectual superiority. Both basked in the intensive media coverage, seeing in it an opportunity to shine in public and outwit their prosecutors. Eventually, both were exposed and the jury found them guilty.

Patrick Hamilton's play *Rope*, filmed by Alfred Hitchcock in 1948, borrows many points from the Leopold and Loeb case. The story is a game of cat and mouse between two precocious and vain students and their former school housemaster, now turned publisher, played by James Stewart. The students murder a fellow student to demonstrate their superior capacity to outwit society, and then conceal the body in a trunk on which they serve a buffet supper to the deceased's family and friends. Rupert Cadell, the character played by Stewart, dines with the boys and gradually exposes the murder. Hitchcock must have been fascinated with the Leopold and Loeb case, because he returned to a similar theme in *Strangers on a Train* (1950).

More recently Ted Bundy, the suave, well-educated serial killer, played a similar game of brinkmanship and staged duplicity with the authorities. Bundy, electrocuted in 1989, never confessed to the full extent of his crimes, but police estimate that he murdered between 20 and 40 women. His victims, all young, were mostly university students of middle- and upper-middle-class status. His motives were unquestionably sexual, but he was also the product of a lower-middle-class family background, in which one's sense of position and place are eternally debated. Even in childhood Bundy appeared to suffer from fraught status anxieties. In captivity, psychiatric investigation concluded that a significant motive in his behaviour was the wish to be caught so as to have a trial that would enable him to confront and outwit figures of authority. At his trial he acted as his own lawyer, and is reported to have behaved with insouciant charm. One psychiatric report maintained that he was obsessed with the public manipulation of authority figures, which he saw in terms of a movie 'thriller', and lacked the capacity to appreciate that the cost of his actions might be his own life. Bundy comes across as a narcissistic figure, full of swagger and bravado, who committed murder and craved celebrity in order to flaunt his approving sense of self-worth before the public.

The most complete expression of the thesis that serial killers kill for pleasure and fame is found in the work of Elliott Leyton.[3] He contends that medical and psychiatric models that portray serial killers as deranged individuals are frequently limited and misleading. He postulates instead that serial killers are often people who seek to break out of the constraining and frustrating lives in which they feel trapped. Plagued by a chronic sense of achievement famine, serial and mass murderers seek to acquire fulfilment in momentary outbursts of aggression coupled with fantasies of the global recognition that will attend their capture.

Noting Jack Katz's observation that homicide is commonly conceived as 'righteous', Leyton argues that killing is often perceived as a triumph or achievement. Capitalist culture proselytizes aggression and condemns emotional repression. Films like *Goodfellas*, *The Usual Suspects*, the *Rambo*, *Lethal Weapon* and *Die Hard* series, TV shows like *NYPD Blue*, *Inspector Morse*, *The Bill* and crime fiction invert Hobbesian contract theory by depicting modern society as a remorseless war of all against all. They are the manifestations of a social order in which the basic cultural codes are competitive individualism, achievement fixation and the narcissistic desire for acclaim. Leyton presents the desire to acquire celebrity status as a powerful motive in modern homicide.

Of course, it is seldom the sole or even the primary motive. Leyton's sociological emphasis on the deformations of acquisitive culture is legitimate. But psychiatrists are also justified in regarding the uncontrollable urge to kill in order to achieve recognition to be a symptom of psychopathology, ego insecurity and low self-esteem. In as much as this is the case, it is often related to an aetiology of family abuse and relative deprivation. Thus the desire to achieve recognition by illegitimate means may be caused by the urge to compensate for a syndrome arising from family or economic position. With regard to David Copeland, it was reported at his trial that, during adolescence, he suffered from taunts of homosexuality in his family, which may have elicited a reaction formation against homosexuals. This approach does not discount the culture of achieved celebrity as a factor in homicidal motivation. Rather, it confirms achieved celebrity as a general desired goal in popular culture, and relates certain types of homicidal behaviour and personality malformation to the pathogenic family.

Many convicted murderers have confessed that they used murder as a vehicle to acquire celebrity. Charles Starkweather, who killed eleven people in 1957–8, refused to offer an insanity plea at his trial on the grounds that society would not remember an insane serial killer. Starkweather identified closely with the screen rebel James Dean, and regarded his murders as revenge on a social system that marginalized his life chances to acquire celebrity by legitimate means. A few years later Arthur Bremer shot Alabama State Governor George Wallace in a self-confessed bid to acquire celebrity, and then worried if Wallace was sufficiently famous to give him the prime-time media coverage he craved. Mark David Chapman, John Lennon's killer, told the US TV interviewer Barbara Walters that 'I thought by killing him I would acquire his fame ... I was Mr Nobody until I killed the biggest somebody on earth'.

Interestingly, the mass-media frequently collude in gratifying the killer's wish for celebrity. For example, the execution of Gary Gilmore in 1977, which followed the reinstitution of the death penalty in America the previous year, was the first state execution in a decade. Over a fourteen-month period, prior to his death by firing squad, Gilmore manipulated the media by refusing legal assistance to commute his sentence to life imprisonment. He successfully overturned the efforts of a Federal judge who had granted a stay of execution at the behest of a group of liberal lawyers, alarmed at the revival of state executions. Gilmore's defence of the right to be executed turned him into a global celebrity. Norman Mailer wrote a voluminous book about the case, *The Executioner's Song*, which was later turned into a movie starring Tommy Lee Jones and Roseanne Arquette.

Mailer was also involved in the release from prison in 1981 of the convicted murderer Jack Henry Abbott. Abbott had written letters to Mailer on the subject of violence and prison life. The novelist judged that the letters possessed literary merit and wrote an article in praise of them. This, together with a sample from the correspondence, was published in *The New York Review of Books*. On the strength of the article Abbott was offered a $12,000 advance by Random House for a full-length book. The book contract, together with strong letters of support from Mailer and Random House, persuaded the parole board to release Abbott. When Abbott's *In the Belly of the Beast* was published soon after, he was fêted by the Manhattan literary elite. Jerzy Kosinski, author of *Being There*, the satire on celebrity later filmed with Peter Sellers in the lead role, and many other books, joined Mailer in praising Abbott's literary talent. Eventually, the book sold over 40,000 hardback copies, producing estimated profits of $500,000 for the author. However, only one month after his release from the Utah State Penitentiary, Abbott stabbed a waiter in a New York restaurant over an apparently trivial argument concerning the use of the washroom. He fled, but after two and a half months on the run was captured, tried and convicted of murder. Like Gilmore, Abbott became a global celebrity. Some interpreted him as a tortured genius who had spent most of his adult life in prison during which he had been the pitiable victim of psychologically damaging humiliation by the authorities. Others dismissed him as an amoral confidence man who ruthlessly manipulated the New York literati to gratify his unquenchable thirst to kill.

One interesting aspect of media collusion with celebrity criminals is the development of the media exclusive interview. Timothy McVeigh, the bomber of the Alfred P. Murrah Federal Building in Oklahoma City, was featured on the cover of *Newsweek* and used the interview to present himself in a favourable light. The interview was part of a campaign developed in conjunction with his attorney to soothe public perceptions of him. McVeigh unsuccessfully petitioned the court to gain the right to a one-hour TV interview with the individual of his choice, from a list that included celebrity interviewers Barbara Walters and Diane Sawyer of ABC, Tom Brokaw of NBC and Dan Rather of CBS. However, somewhat controversially, the court agreed to relay his execution live on CCTV to families of the victims of the Alfred P. Murrah bombing.

McVeigh was not the only notorious figure of contemporary times to present his celebrity as a *cause célèbre*. Theodore Kaczynski, the so-called 'Unabomber', delivered an ultimatum to *The New York Times* to publish his manifesto, otherwise he would kill again. Kaczynski revealed himself to be image-conscious, and concerned to manage the details of his elevation in public culture so that his reputation and claim to immortality would be correctly appreciated. For Neal Gabler, both McVeigh and Kaczynski behaved like celebrities promoting a new movie.[4] After presenting their 'achievement' to the public, they craved prime time to expound and exonerate their 'heroic' behaviour.

In the UK, where arguably the cult of individualism is weaker than in America, killer celebrities do not possess equivalent media cachet. This is not to say that the British are immune to the media presentation of celebrity killers, or that killers refrain from murdering to gain recognition.

In the 1960s a significant cult of celebrity developed around the notorious Kray twins. Ron and Reggie Kray's crime empire was based in London's East End. They presented themselves as working-class heroes. The milieu in which they grew up recognized crime and boxing as the quickest routes to fame and fortune. The twins developed a network of contacts with London film celebrities, Pop singers and sportsmen, notably boxers. They mixed glamour with violence and extortion. They self-consciously mythologized themselves. They kept scrapbooks of their criminal exploits and boxing triumphs. Ronnie Kray was fascinated with the tough-guy image of the Chicago gangster, and sought to emulate it in his dress and public behaviour. In the East End the Krays ruled their territory with greater authority than the police. They symbolized the traditional camaraderie of East End life, and they claimed to look after the old, the infirm and the needy. Popular myth had it that the East End's streets were safer under the Krays than they had ever been. Of course, what this ignored was the systematic network of violence that regulated behaviour through intimidation, threats and assault.

George Orwell, in a famous essay on the decline of the English murder, maintained that national characteristics differentiate the classical English murder from those of other nations.[5] Thus, he argued, the English murder is generally premeditated and requires careful attention to detail. The motive is typically split between lust and avarice. The murderer is usually male, and kills his wife in order to be with his mistress and inherit the house and savings, or cash in on stocks or the insurance policy. Orwell reasoned, perhaps somewhat fatuously, that the English take murder to be less shameful than adultery. The exposure of the murderer is generally a slow process, where providence eventually reveals an unforeseeable slip in the planning. When these details are in place, argued Orwell, the murder has the necessary dramatic and tragic qualities to make it memorable and to engender pity for both the victim and the murderer. For Orwell, the golden age of the English murder roughly covers the period 1850–1925.

Celebrity killers of that era include Dr Palmer of Rugely, Jack the Ripper, Dr Crippen, Neill Cream and Edith Thompson and Frederick Bywaters.

Orwell's argument was, in fact, a cleverly disguised attack on British insularity and bourgeois insecurity, and a squib against Americanization. He proposed that the English murder was in danger of being swamped by American values of spontaneous violence and immediate gratification. As an example, he referred to the so-called 'Cleft-Chin Murder' of his own day, in which an American army deserter and an English striptease dancer, apparently in search of excitement, engaged in an unpremeditated rout of assault and murder in October 1944. The press in Britain, sensitive to the threat of Americanization yet not wishing to put Anglo-American relations under strain at a critical moment in the Second World War, presented the murderers as amoral products of consumer culture, driven by a search for the ultimate high in immediate gratification.

The facetious tone in Orwell's essay, which is apparent in his support for the preservation of traditional values in respect of murder, suggests that he was being mischievous. Be that as it may, the thesis has been falsified by post-war trends. In both Britain and the US, spontaneous murder 'for kicks' is actually comparatively rare.

Similarly, outbursts of mass aggression directed against anonymous victims, such as the Hungerford (1987), Dunblane (1996) and Soho (1999) massacres, perpetrated respectively by Michael Ryan, Thomas Hamilton and David Copeland, periodically renew moral panics in the media, alleging that contemporary culture is sliding towards a state of complete anarchy and amorality. But they are still statistically negligible in wider patterns of homicide. Most murder victims and murderers are related by kinship or marriage ties. None the less, Leyton maintains that the incidence of spectacular mass and serial killings is increasing; and further, that celebrity culture is causally significant in increasing the trend. A strain of modern killer has emerged who slaughters for public recognition and the acquisition of notoriety.

Of course, it would be an error to infer that all mass murder and serial killing can be adequately explained as a quest for notoriety. The point at issue is merely that this line of enquiry helps to explain a significant strain in contemporary homicide. The importance of the proposition here is that it implies that in some cases, where achievement famine is regarded to be insurmountable, notoriety may be pursued as a strategy for gaining public recognition. Notoriety may be additionally defined as 'unfavourable celebrity'. It demonstrates the acknowledgement of achievement famine in the life of the perpetrator, and the wish to acquire public recognition, albeit of an unfavourable kind. But for some people notoriety is coveted since it affords them instant public recognition and fame.

The Anti-Hero

Notoriety is not necessarily pursued for self-aggrandizement. The acquisition of unfavourable celebrity may be pursued as a strategy to expose a state of affairs in society perceived as unsatisfactory. This is frequently the motive attributed to the anti-hero in Western culture. The anti-hero lacks conventional heroic characteristics because the veridical self is stigmatized by society, and therefore does not receive the rewards that accrue to the conventional hero. Stigmatization may arise because the individual occupies a lowly status in the social hierarchy, or because the values he expresses are anathema to society.

When Mark David Chapman shot John Lennon, he claimed to be following instructions contained in J. D. Salinger's cult novel *The Catcher in the Rye* (1951). This extraordinary, compelling narrative of an American anti-hero has been an enduring favourite with readers, especially adolescents, for half a century. Doubtless Salinger's own unyielding reclusiveness has added to the mystique of the novel. He has published only a trickle of other writings, and maintains a ferocious code of privacy by vetoing the publication of photographs of himself, avoiding public appearances and seeking to suppress newsworthy items. Salinger is the antithesis of the publicity-hungry novelist. Other popular novelists, for example John Updike, Saul Bellow, Salman Rushdie, Philip Roth, Jeanette Winterson, Martin Amis, Peter Carey, Tom Wolfe and Jay McInerney, regularly participate in interviews, symposia, chat shows, signing sessions and volunteer public readings to plug their work. By contrast, Salinger remains aloof from the publishing publicity machine and prefers to allow his work to speak for itself.

Holden Caulfield, the protagonist in *The Catcher in the Rye*, is the classic fictional anti-hero of post-war literature. He is alienated from the values of respectable society. He regards them as lacking honesty. They obey the mechanical requirements of social responsibility rather than the imperative of authentic feeling. Rather as in T. S. Eliot's poem *The Hollow Men* (1925), society is pictured as a collection of 'hollow', 'stuffed' men who lean together, 'headpieces filled with straw'. Salinger's novel celebrates integrity, even at the cost of disrupting social and cultural order. If *The Catcher in the Rye* is one of the most powerful fictional treatments of the anti-hero, one may venture that Salinger's rejection of celebrity culture makes him the leading embodiment of the anti-hero among contemporary novelists.

Randle P. McMurphy, the lead character in Ken Kesey's novel *One Flew Over the Cuckoo's Nest* (1962), is another prophetic anti-hero whose rebellion in a lunatic asylum was celebrated by 1960s counter culture and the anti-psychiatry movement. The conflict between McMurphy and the authoritarian Nurse Ratched cleverly dramatizes the irrational consequences of rational organization. McMurphy emerges as a sane rebel trapped in an insane and ultimately ruthless system. (Jack Nicholson's portrayal of McMurphy, filmed by Milos Forman in 1975, is acknowledged to be one of the best dramatizations of the anti-hero in cinema.)

Market society rewards achievement with esteem and wealth. But if these values are ultimately illusory, as Marx, Weber and Freud maintained, the aspirations, convictions and dreams of capitalist culture must be hallucinations. The anti-hero may be defined as an individual who perceives the codes and mores governing respectable culture as hallucinations. Violence is frequently the means employed by the anti-hero to break hallucinatory structures of power. Travis Bickle, played by Robert De Niro in Martin Scorsese's lacerating attack on the values of 1970s New York, *Taxi Driver* (1976), regards himself to be the only sensitive, noble individual left in a city of desensitized, acquisitive drones. By electing to champion the teenage prostitute, played by Jodie Foster, and annihilate the gang of pimps and confidence men who oppress her, Travis seeks to retrieve morality. The film historian David Thomson has compared the scene in which De Niro straps guns and knives to his body and shaves his head into a Mohican cut to 'a saint in flagellation'. There is certainly great power in the final fifteen minutes of the film, in which Travis exterminates the brothel keepers and pimps in a frenzy of righteous slaughter. Yet as Thomson concludes, 'film and dream have no more ominous or transcendent moment than that in *Taxi Driver* when Travis survives his pitched battle, returns as a hero, but still presents a haunted face to his own rear-view mirror.'[6] The anti-hero, then, wages a doomed battle to redeem society, because society has set its face towards immediate gratification, hedonism and Mammon. Protest is, finally, useless. The search for authenticity is a gesture to a submerged moral world engulfed by the incessant commercialism and artificial titillation of consumer culture.

The anti-hero is a recurring theme in Hollywood film. Other famous examples include James Dean in *Rebel Without a Cause* (1955), Marlon Brando in *The Wild One* (1953), Warren Beatty in *Bonnie & Clyde* (1967) and Al Pacino in *Serpico* (1973). Clint Eastwood has been typecast in the role in a series of successful Westerns – *A Fistful of Dollars* (1964), *The Good, the Bad, and the Ugly* (1967), *High Plains Drifter* (1973), *The Outlaw Josey Wales* (1976) and *Unforgiven* (1992). The concept of the anti-hero is closely connected with the concept of righteous slaughter.

Righteous Slaughter

In arguing that 'the modal criminal homicide is an impassioned attempt to perform a sacrifice to embody one or another version of the 'Good', Jack Katz retrieved the concept of 'righteous slaughter' from the aesthetic level and situated it in concrete social relations.[7] Katz is defending the proposition that a plea for rational justice is often a motivation in violent crime. This proposition is frequently neglected in media reports and public perceptions that tend to be preoccupied by the presentation of violent acts as 'random' or 'crazy'. Katz's argument is that killers generally murder for a reason, and that their self-image typically consists of an anti-hero avenging a perceived humiliation or injustice.

A new element has been added by Elliott Leyton, who proposes that the righteous slaughter waged by mass and serial killers is also an attempt to acquire celebrity. The media presentation of these kinds of killing often assumes a flamboyant, cinematic style. This is also perhaps part of the mind-set of the perpetrator. As the discussion of David Copeland and Ted Bundy intimated, the killer regards himself to be playing the starring role in his own movie, and often wishes to be caught so as to acquire celebrity status and test out a sense of self-regard in public.

Part of the mythology of the anti-hero is that the values he adheres to are so polarized from ordinary society that they cannot be communicated or understood by others. In as much as society is perceived as being prey to hallucinatory beliefs, convictions and habits, the only option to the anti-hero is to turn poacher. Further, even if the poaching instinct is appeased, there is no guarantee of recognition. Where the anti-hero concludes that the act of righteous slaughter will be judged as 'pathological' or 'meaningless', suicide may emerge as the preferred option. In some cases, serial or mass killing may culminate in suicide. This was the case with Michael Ryan, the Hungerford murderer, and Thomas Hamilton, the Dunblane killer. On the other hand, the potential mass or serial killer may conclude that suicide is preferable to being wrongly acknowledged. The killer perceives himself to be a tragic anti-hero whose righteous revenge against perceived humiliation and injustice will be fatefully mistranslated by society.

A case in point is the mass murderer Mark James Robert Essex, discussed by Leyton. According to media reports of the time, Essex was a social misfit who conducted a one-man war against the city of New Orleans in eight days of mayhem. The facts seem unequivocal. Between New Year's Eve and 7 January 1974, Essex shot dead ten people, wounded 23 and caused millions of dollars of damage to property. Essex knew none of the victims. On the contrary, he seemed to have selected them at random. The killings did not involve theft or rape. For the white-dominated mass-media, Essex was the quintessence of the deranged killer. However, as Leyton demonstrates, careful consideration of the facts elicits a contrasting, more plausible interpretation. To begin with, a clear and unambiguous racial motive lay behind the killings. Essex was black. True, he killed a black person inadvertently in his slaying spree, but his target was whites.

Second, far from being an indiscriminate killer, Essex targeted authority figures and sites. His first attack was directed against the New Orleans police department's Central Lockup. He lit fires in city warehouses in an attempt to draw the police into open spaces. When this failed he broke into a downtown hotel, fired at white security staff, killing one, and set alight a room on the eighteenth floor. The conflagration drew firefighters and police to the scene of the crime. Eventually over 600 policemen from Louisiana, Texas and Mississippi, as well as FBI and military personnel, were called out.

Third, the manner of Essex's last, and fatal, stand suggests a deliberate intention to create an event worthy of national, even global, mass-media coverage. He deliberately sought to face impossible odds. It was not a battle, it was an act of staged public suicide. Essex evidently regarded the murders he committed, and his death, to possess transcendent symbolic significance. He killed, and was killed, to make a point.

Nothing in Essex's childhood gave reason to suggest that he would grow up to be a mass murderer. Leyton describes his upbringing as 'thoughtful', 'progressive', 'non-violent' and 'non-racist'. His father worked as a foreman in a small family-owned company. The children were encouraged to think of themselves as upwardly mobile. Yet, in Essex's case, fate intervened. In 1969 he volunteered for the US Navy, in a bid to escape the Vietnam draft. Initial training identified him as an outstanding recruit. Eventually he opted to train as a dental technician. Again he was successful. His supervisor identified him as 'promising'. Essex dreamed of entering the professional class as a dentist.

The public face that Essex felt impelled to construct did in fact mask a deeply wounded veridical self. He suffered racial discrimination that served as the tinder-box to the sense of indignity and persecution beginning to oppress him. He rebelled. He struck a white Petty Officer in an argument. He was summonsed for court martial, went absent without leave, but voluntarily returned for trial. Leyton describe the trial as 'Kafkaesque'. Essex was found guilty of responding to racial harassment, ordered to forfeit pay for two months, confined to barracks and downgraded to a lower pay scale. In short order, he was advised to apply for 'administrative discharge' on the grounds that he was unsuitable for continued service in the Navy.

Thereafter, for the interim at least, Essex becomes an enigma. He leaves the Navy, and is evidently humiliated by the reasons for his departure. What is known is that he returns to his family and sporadically visits New Orleans and New York on mystery trips, which he justifies as 'visits to old Navy friends'. He begins to amass black revolutionary writings. Police reports identify contact with the Black Panther movement and rogue black militants who become 'significant others'. Gradually he develops the self-image of a race warrior. Essex grows increasingly self-absorbed and segregated from the means of re-entering society at a level that he deems appropriate to his intelligence and achievements. He becomes angry, at first in a sub-clinical way, but slowly with a fatal compulsion that he is unable to resist. He decides, not unreasonably, that his rejection by the Navy, and his marginalized predicament, reflects deep-seated white racism.

Self-absorption and anger often elicit the conclusion that the veridical self is at fault in suffering from achievement famine. The qualities of the veridical self are not sufficiently recognized by others, so certain individuals reason that the veridical self is, to some degree, unworthy. It is rationalized thus: either the veridical self is too good for this world, or that communication of reality with others is impossible. In such circumstances, anger may be directed inwards, resulting in the decision to extinguish the self, in what Durkheim famously called 'egoistic suicide'.

Essex is known to have been a serious and sensitive young man. Several characteristics of his behaviour between leaving the Navy and the shootings suggest suicidal intentions. He was isolated, listless and burdened by overwhelming feelings of under-achievement. However, instead of regarding these to be intrinsic faults in the veridical self, he rationalized them as the consequences of white intimidation. By 1974 Essex existed in a psychological milieu permeated with the unpalatable fact of white domination. The routes for upward mobility that might have elevated him out of his situation seemed closed to him. In any case, by 1974 he concluded that to be an upwardly mobile black man was part of the problem, not the solution. His thoughts fastened on arousing black culture from its lethargy. Specifically, he decided to dramatize his own humiliation and degradation in an act of social protest and racial incitement. From this perspective, his death can be interpreted as an example of 'altruistic suicide', i.e., self-extinction for the good of the collectivity. In facing the massed ranks of the armed, repressive apparatus of the white state, Essex believed that he sacrificed himself to challenge the inhuman condition of white domination. The highly public, drawn-out manner of his last stand suggests an intention to transform his death into a plea for celebrity recognition. But it was recognition on behalf of the oppressed black population rather than personal aggrandizement.

The Columbine High School massacre in the Denver suburb of Littleton provides a parallel example. On 20 April 1999, Eric Harris, aged eighteen, and Dylan Klebold, seventeen, shot dead twelve schoolmates and a teacher and wounded 23 others before both committed suicide. They left behind no notes or explanations. Both were students from apparently stable, relatively prosperous homes. Apart from a year on probation for breaking into an automobile, they had no record of violent or criminal behaviour. During probation, each received positive reports on their intelligence and sincerity from the counselling service. At first, their reasons for carrying out the massacre seemed a mystery.

Police inquiries established that the two belonged to a small gang subculture in the school known as the 'Trench Coat Mafia', who adopted the style of the so-called 'Dark Wave'. This consisted of Right-wing music, a fixation with death, and a preference for dark funereal clothes, white make-up and jet-black lipstick. Harris and Klebold were known to be fans of techno, the electronic music of rave events, and the German industrial rock band Rammstein, who have been accused of endorsing neo-Nazi values in their lyrics. Both also followed Gothick rock, produced by groups like Skrewdriver, Razors Edge, Nordic Thunder, Brutal Attack and Aggravated Assault, whose lyrics have been criticized for preaching white supremacy, inciting violence and race hatred. In addition, as with other members of the Trench Coat Mafia, Harris and Klebold were taunted by classmates for showing an unhealthy interest in Nazism. The press noted that 20 April, the day of the massacre, was also Hitler's birthday.

The main proponents of mockery and teasing against the Trench Coat Mafia were the jock crowd. Spectators who witnessed the massacre reported that the gunmen asked several students if they were part of that crowd before deciding whether to kill them. The media speculated that the killings might have been some sort of revenge against the values of straight society.

Eric Harris's website, which used the screen name 'Rebdomine', gave reason to believe that he was deeply alienated from straight society. It included drawings of devils, guns and pyres of skulls. One of his poems, clearly drawing lavishly on the imagery of the Dark Wave, suggests profound antagonism against 'normal' culture:

I have come to rock your world
I have come to shake your faith
　　anathematic antichrist
I have come to take my place
I am your unconsciousness
I am unrestrained excess
metamorphic restlessness
I'm your unexpectedness
I am your apocalypse
I am your belief unwrought
monolithic juggernaut
I'm the illegitimate son of God
Shockwave
Massive attack
Atomic blast
Son of a gun is back
Chaos-panic
No resistance
Detonations in the distance
Apocalypse now
Walls of flame
Billowing smoke

Who's to blame
Forged from steel
Iron will
Shit for brains
Born to kill
All are equal
No discrimination
Son of a gun
A simple equation
Son of a gun
Matter of fate
Bows to no God, kingdom or
    state
Watch out
Son of a gun
Superhero number 1
If you don't like it, well ...
    you know what to do
Anything I don't like – SUCKS.

But to read too much into this is, perhaps, to be wise after the event. David Copeland also dreamt of apocalyptic change in British society. So do many youths who confront the difficult *rite de passage* into adult society. Most, like their parents before them, overcome this hurdle.

What made Harris, Klebold and Copeland unable to take this step is, of course, the decisive question. The rather courageous 'Tears for Eric and Dylan' website depicts the killers not as cyphers or as media monsters but as 'bright', 'funny', 'misjudged', 'misunderstood' teenage boys in pain. The site pleads for an understanding of school harassment and the misperception of teachers. It invites us to see Harris and Klebold as victims of society, rather than as mindless murderers.

But there are, needless to say, other ways of protesting against harassment than mass murder. The manner of the Columbine massacre, with its frenzy of killing and the network of explosive devices planted in the school grounds, suggests that Harris and Klebold were intent on creating a spectacular incident that would poleaxe the mass-media into global coverage. They cast themselves in the starring role of perpetrators in a moral outrage. The Second Surrealist Manifesto, one of the most artful expressions of modern aesthetics, asserted that 'the simplest Surrealist act consists in going revolver in hand, into the street and firing as much as possible at random into the crowd'.[8] Harris and Klebold may have known about the aesthetics of Surrealism, but they were hardly disciples of André Breton, Salvador Dalí and Tristan Tzara. They understood the value of spectacle, because as babies born within twelve months on either side of the Falklands War, their first consciousness of global warfare was the Gulf War (1991), whose 'smart bombs' seemed to disassociate killing from pain. They did not kill merely as victims of society, they killed as aspirants for global celebrity, by means of a spectacular act of violence. However, what the 'Tears for Eric and Dylan' website does successfully convey is the vulnerability of the pair. They were susceptible to delusions of white supremacy and the righteous revenge of the anti-hero because they suffered gross acts of intimidation and because they had grown up in a culture that glorifies righteous revenge. As males they found it difficult to externalize their vulnerability by seeking help from qualified counsellors or psychotherapists. Instead, they pooled their individual frustration with each other, and made a pact to translate their pain into a *cause célèbre* through an act of spectacular transgression.

Transgression, then, is a tried and tested route in the acquisition of notoriety. It enables individuals who experience achievement famine to gain media recognition and public status as singular or enlarged personalities. From the standpoint of the anti-hero, notoriety is a legitimate goal, since the values of society are rejected on *a priori* grounds as hallucinatory.

The incidence of serial and mass murder is widely believed to be increasing. Perhaps one can postulate a rationale in social conditions where achievement famine is generalized and the culture of achievement pre-eminent. From this one might infer that notoriety is becoming a more common means of acquiring public recognition. To some extent the mass-media collude in this process by representing the pseudo-event and the celetoid as worthy objects of public attention. Where individuals cannot acquire achievement through legitimate means there will be a tendency for some to resort to illegitimate means to gain public recognition.

The argument points to an ambiguity in society's attitudes to right-eous revenge. It is correct to maintain that all forms of society censure homicide. At the same time, Western law recognizes the concept of miti-gating circumstances, which allows for provocation or mental instability to be taken into account in the judgement of an individual's criminal behaviour. In England and Wales the so-called 'McNaughton Rules' of 1843 established insanity as a legitimate defence in the trial of homicide. Daniel McNaughton was tried for the murder of Edward Drummond, private secretary to Prime Minister Sir Robert Peel, under the delusion that he was shooting Peel himself. McNaughton was acquitted on the grounds of insanity. This led to the incorporation of the notion of 'diminished responsibility' into English law. Diminished responsibility recognizes that society acknowledges mental illness as a legitimate form of defence to be tested through criminal trial. Of course, in the eyes of the anti-hero the standpoint of society is beside the point, since the purpose of violent action is to expose the hallucinatory character of dominant social values in order to achieve public recognition. However, the legal acceptance of notions of diminished responsibility and miti-gating circumstances supports the hypothesis that righteous revenge is culturally significant in the aetiology of crime. For it acknowledges that the censure of violent crime must take account of the mental and emotional circumstances in which crime is committed. Of course, what provokes someone to kill remains a matter of the interweaving of precise bio-chemical, psychological and sociological factors. But the culture of contemporary society is a legitimate factor to consider in determining diminished responsibility.

The evidence in support of Leyton's thesis is inconclusive. It may be tenable to propose that the condition of achievement famine and the culture of righteous revenge elicits a propensity in some individuals to use violent crime to achieve notoriety. On the other hand, achievement famine does not automatically or universally bear this result. Further, the cases of mass murder and serial killing in which achievement famine is a plausible causal factor in behaviour are quite rare. This is not to discount the symbolic significance of achievement famine in shaping everyday behaviour. Frustration and resentment at a lack of recognition in work or family relations abounds in contemporary society. However, comparatively speaking, the cognitive dissonance that accrues from this condition seldom results in suicide or aggressive outbursts directed against others.

Conversely, the concept of righteous revenge is often a prominent defence in acts of homicide. The notion that the culture of righteous revenge, associated with Hollywood films such as *Death Wish* (1974), *Taxi Driver* (1976) and the *Die Hard* series, supports a tendency to resort to illegitimate means to acquire public recognition is tenable. However, one must remember that the 'right to murder' is a tenuous motive, and requires detailed medical, psychological and sociological exposition before it can be legally recognized.

The Charm of Notoriety

The connection between notoriety and transgression has been long appreciated and extensively explored in bohemian culture. Erving Goffman, while noting that unfavourable celebrity is usually stigmatized, acknowledged that deviation can be developed as a positive life strategy geared to the acquisition of status.[9] He recognized that denial of the social order possesses social cachet, most notably in bohemian circles. As examples, he lists criminals, jazz musicians, show people and full-time gamblers.

Why should this type of social actor receive honorific status? Social deviance involves going beyond the role boundaries that govern ordinary social interaction. Often it involves breaking the law and causing mental or physical harm to the self and others. In his autobiography Miles Davis recalls his teenage fascination with jazz players like Dizzy Gillespie and Charlie Parker. Davis, who eventually became a heroin addict himself, was drawn to the bohemian jazz lifestyle, with its emphasis on liberation, drugs and casual sex. But what entranced him about the lifestyle of the jazz musician was the transformative capacity of playing music in public. As he wrote of Charlie 'Bird' Parker: 'Bird changed the minute he put his horn in his mouth ... he went from looking real down and out to having all his power and beauty just bursting out of him. It was amazing the transformation that took place once he started playing.'[10] The capacity to go beyond yourself, to be taken outside of the routine constraints and responsibilities that govern role performance in ordinary social life, is immensely seductive. Alcohol and drugs are common means of achieving transgression. Davis notes that Parker was often drunk or stoned on stage. The addicted genius, who experiments with alcohol and drugs as a way of escaping from the constraining boundaries of ordinary social interaction, is a powerful motif in Romantic culture. But the figure of the cultural transgressor, who rejects ordinary social values as over-limiting in the cultivation of social form and experiments in the altered states of drink and drugs, is both celebrated and reviled in ordinary social life.

The Marquis de Sade is a pivotal decadent figure for the Age of Enlightenment. He was an aristocratic voluptuary who achieved notoriety through sexual cruelty. Richard von Krafft-Ebing, the noted nineteenth-century German neurologist, derived the term *sadism* from the name of the Marquis, to describe sexual pleasure gained by inflicting pain on others. Perhaps de Sade is misrepresented as solely a sadist, because masochism was an equally important element in his sexual orientation. Be that as it may, he pitted himself against the standardizing, the levelling down of personality and practice demanded by the French Revolution. His reputation as a sexual deviant became mixed with the anti-heroic status of a rebel against bureaucratic society.

Lord Byron gained a similar reputation as a libertine and rebel, although he was never quite in de Sade's league as a voluptuary and transgressor. His notoriety lay in the scandals that surrounded his life – whoring, adultery, incest and sodomy. But his romantic legend derived from the gauntlet he flung in the face of respectable society, and his death in the cause of the Greek War of Independence. Byron's notoriety was deemed to be sufficiently scandalous to threaten polite society, so that on his death his publisher, John Murray, took it on himself to incinerate the two bound manuscript volumes containing Byron's handwritten memoirs.

Byron and de Sade were aristocrats, and bearers of ascribed status. The notoriety they achieved through their exploits in moral and cultural transgression gained them achieved notoriety that eclipsed their ascribed celebrity. Neither was popularly understood as a class warrior. Both gained enduring fame as maverick individuals whose writings and lifestyles condemned public morality. In the nineteenth century the opportunities for achieved celebrity increased. The culture of achieved notoriety also grew as aesthetic, sexual and political rebels challenged the prevailing public moral order. Baudelaire, for example, famously cultivated the persona of a bohemian dandy. He dyed his hair green, claimed to own a book bound in human skin, affected to be a cannibal of infants, and confessed in his journals to be intoxicated by the aristocratic pleasure of displeasing. *Les Fleurs du mal* was impounded on publication in 1857, and Baudelaire was prosecuted for offending public morality. Six poems were incriminated and, by court order, removed from the book. Baudelaire was fined 300 francs. The prosecution only served to contribute to his notoriety as an anti-hero. Interestingly, he was critical of the use of hashish and opium to stimulate artistic invention. He believed that drugs both flattered and debased the imagination. By implication, the celebrated drug-induced writings of Coleridge and De Quincey are regarded to be inferior versions of 'real' art. However, Baudelaire's hostility to narcotics is partly belied by his own dependence on absinthe, a dependence that Oscar Wilde also developed during his ignominious exile in Paris.

Aleister Crowley, the notorious poet, magician, pornographer and heroin addict who scandalized Edwardian England, also developed a cult following among those who regarded conventional moral and cultural boundaries as too limiting. His 'magick' sought to synthesize oriental esoteric techniques, Golden Dawn magic and sexual sorcery with the all-encompassing 'Law of Thelema'. The last-named was founded on two principles that may be regarded as the bedrock of notorious celebrity in the twentieth century: 'Every man and woman is a star'; and 'Do What Thou Wilt Shall be the Whole of the Law'. Crowley's 'magick' invested every man and woman with cosmic significance and authorized them to question and transgress moral and cultural precepts he maintained limited social form unduly.

On the whole, transgression and the cultivation of notoriety as a life strategy have been easier for men than women. The Empress Josephine famously made a cuckold of Napoleon by openly taking a series of lovers and initiating a series of sexual scandals in Paris. Napoleon eventually divorced her, and although she received a degree of emotional and financial support from him, she was socially disgraced.

The silent film star Louise Brooks epitomized the liberated 'new woman' or 'flapper' of F. Scott Fitzgerald's 'Jazz Age'. But she defied studio injunctions to adhere to the moral code of the silent majority. Her attitude was openly sexually calculating. Long-term commitment did not figure in her scheme of things. She believed that 'all men hate women' and wrote:

> Quite early in life I learned to pay attention to what I *did* and not what I *thought*. I would say to myself I am not going to get drunk and lay this bastard and all the time I would be filling my purse, not with the Cartier cigarette case and compact which I might lose drunk, but with lesser items. Or I would have a date with some man who might do me good saying to myself I am going to be enchanting and flattering, all the while rehearsing the vicious truths I would hurl at him.[11]

Brooks's distinction between action and thought should perhaps be read as an early feminist *cri de coeur*. Phallocentric society places intense pressure on women to separate the public face from the veridical self. In the case of the female celebrity, the pressure upon the veridical self is subject to a syndrome of double estrangement. The celebrity is separated from her true feelings by the social obligations of gender division, and alienated by public expectations of the celebrity face that the veridical self may interpret as impertinent or annihilating. Thus the female celebrity may be said to lead a life in triplex – the person she is, the person male conquests think she is, and the public face.

For Brooks, promiscuity was arguably a way of managing feelings of double estrangement. Her list of lovers was as long as that of the leading male stars of the day. The difference was that, for the most part, the erotic life of male stars was permitted to flourish with half-hearted censure, while

Brooks was castigated as a moral leper. Hollywood producers despised her intelligence and wrecked her film career. She fell into the oblivion of alcoholism, poverty and prostitution, and was only rediscovered by film enthusiasts in the last years of her life.

Frances Farmer inherited the public mantle of Brooks in the late 1930s. But her public presence as a film star spanned six years, between 1936 and 1941. A student from the University of Washington, Farmer gained critical acclaim in Howard Hawks's *Come and Get It* (1936), a film completed by William Wyler after Hawks was fired. She went on to play in undistinguished films, the mediocrity of which intensified her problems with alcohol and relationships with men. Farmer's behaviour became increasingly unpredictable, wayward and disturbing. Eventually, she was institutionalized and lobotomized. In feminist film circles she is revered as the Randle P. McMurphy of her day. She resurfaced in the late 1950s in a couple of TV movies, but slipped into obscurity, dying prematurely in 1970 at the age of 56. Jessica Lange received an Oscar nomination for her portrayal of Farmer in Graeme Clifford's film *Frances* (1982).

Notoriety is often associated with shifts in aesthetic culture. When John Ruskin viewed James Whistler's *Nocturnes* he famously denigrated the painter for 'flinging a pot of paint in the public's face'. This was pleading in defence of the traditional values of fine art which, he believed, Whistler's paintings violated. The resultant libel case found in Whistler's favour but awarded him only one farthing damages and refused costs. The derisory award reflected the jury's belief that Whistler was technically right to complain of libel, and perversely vindicated Ruskin's judgement. The incident destabilized the authority of fine art values, and raised the debate about the nature of art.

Marcel Duchamp's entire career can be interpreted as an investigation into the question *What is art?* His painting *Nude Descending a Staircase* provoked disbelief and rage when it was included in the International Exhibition of Modern Art in 1913. The painting seemed to bear no relation to human form, and Duchamp was suspected of exposing the poverty of Cubism. But this was as nothing compared to the furore that erupted in 1917, at the Society of Independent Artists Show, when Duchamp, using the alias 'R. Mutt', submitted a flat-back 'Bedfordshire' porcelain urinal as an exhibit under the title *Fountain*. Duchamp was partly engaged in a sally against the stuffy elite values of fine art critics. But he was also emphasizing the ubiquity of aestheticization in everyday life, a point taken up and developed by the Surrealists, notably Breton, Dalí and Man Ray. This theme continues in contemporary art. Robert Mapplethorpe's sexually explicit, homo-erotic photographs, Andres Serrano's *Piss Christ* and *Milk Blood* and Karen Finley's 'body art' performances have attracted accusations of 'degeneracy'. Such work questions the meaning of decency and reality, but it also reflects the role that the contemporary artist plays in cultivating notoriety.

Notoriety, then, is both a way of achieving personal celebrity and of gaining public recognition of a transformation in culture. Often the two are conflated. Oscar Wilde's championing of the new Aesthetic Movement between the 1870s and 1890s was clearly also a means of publicizing himself as a celebrity figure. Dalí pursued a similar course in his relations with the Surrealist movement in the 1920s and '30s. Robert Mapplethorpe and Andres Serrano are more recent cases in point. Careers of achieved celebrity built around notoriety are difficult to sustain. The pressure on the individual is to produce one outrage after the other, so that the effect of diminishing returns sets in.

This chapter has argued that celebrity is inherently bound up with transgression. There are three reasons for this. First, celebrity divides the individual from ordinary social life. To be a celebrity is to be recognized as different. The enlargement of choice and the flexibility of lifestyle are both attractive and problematic. Celebrities have more money, more property and more sexual and social opportunities than ordinary people, but they frequently complain of feeling trapped and prey to the 'achievement mirage' syndrome.

This brings me to my second point. Celebrity is based in the assembly of a public face that necessarily alters the veridical self. Cary Grant, who started life in Bristol as Archie Leach, constantly returned to the friction between the public face and the veridical self. For much of his career, Grant's public face concealed profound anxieties about the mortification of Archie Leach. As he put it, 'I had a lot of problems over the years, but they were Archie Leach's problems, not Cary Grant's.'[12] Grant's decision to take LSD at the end of the 1950s seems to have reconciled some of these problems. At the time, LSD treatment was a Government-licensed experiment. Grant estimated that he underwent about 100 sessions over a three-year period. The treatment seems to have had a therapeutic effect. Grant regarded it to be the catalyst in the *rapprochement* between his public face and veridical self. 'I spent the greater part of my life fluctuating between Archie Leach and Cary Grant', he recalled, 'unsure of either, suspecting each. Then I began to unify them into one person. With unity came peace and relaxation.'[13]

Third, the contradiction between the desire to achieve celebrity and the limited means of goal attainment creates a propensity in culture for individuals to resort to illegitimate means to acquire recognition. Obviously, not everybody in culture wants to be a celebrity. On the other hand, the kudos attached to achieved celebrity demonstrably possesses high cultural value. Democratic culture is necessarily an achievement culture. Theoretically, democracy is founded in the annulment of the monarchical principle and treats all citizens as equal before the law. Through public education and the welfare state, democracy offers each individual the chance of social ascent. Pre-eminence is decided in accordance with individual merit. Might one propose that part of the psychological allure of celebrity, no less than the temptations of notoriety, resides in the gap between the theory and practice of democracy? In as much as this is so, are celebrity and notoriety a response to both the absence of religion and the practical limitations of democratic culture? As I noted at the start of this book, celebrity culture was born in the age of the common man. In public culture, and the recognition of democracy over feudalism and communism, the achieved celebrity is born. It is fitting, then, that my final chapter should address the relationship between the age of the common man (democracy) and the inexorable celebrification process (distinction).

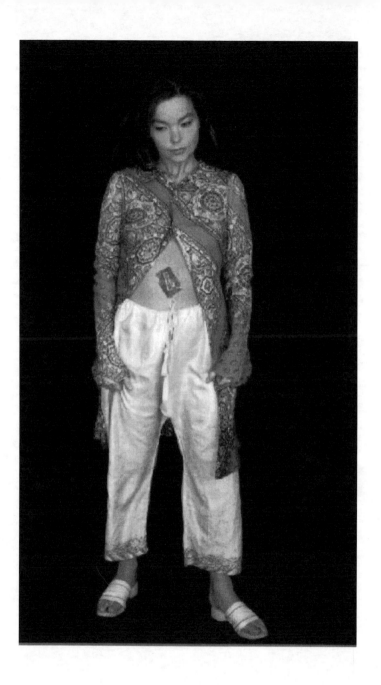

CHAPTER FIVE

Celebrity and Celebrification

Democracy perpetually fails to deliver what it promises, and arguably, this failure is most cruelly exposed in the limitations of its elected leaders. There are many reasons for this, but two are of relevance here. First, democratically elected leaders are not assigned to power by virtue of tradition or military fiat. On the contrary, they are the freely chosen representatives of popular will. In being elected by the people, and holding office for the people, presidents and prime ministers embody the prestige vested in them by the posited superiority of democracy over monarchy and totalitarianism. They are the perpetual objects of media scrutiny and enjoy special media privileges to communicate with the public. In the political sphere, they are the ultimate achieved celebrities.

Second, because they are drawn from the ranks of the people they are expected to embody the virtues of the people. Traditionally, presidents and prime ministers are the central symbolic figures in post-monarchical society, who enable individuals to understand each other and themselves. In being the ultimate achieved celebrities of the political sphere, they demonstrate that any individual can aspire to the highest office in the land. In advanced urban–industrial society, democracy is necessarily a mediated mass process. Data-gathering, policy formation, policing and administration involves a vast bureaucratic salariat. Presidents and prime ministers personalize democracy by constructing the public face by which the salariat is recognized and evaluated. For this reason the failings of a president or a prime minister have ubiquitous repercussions affecting the mental and emotional life of the nation.

On what basis does democracy's claim of superiority rest? In societies in which there is no transcendent foundation of values, democracy appears to be the only plausible base for authority. If God, monarchy and tyranny are dead, the only eligible system of government is democracy, in which elected representatives of the people are publicly charged with the task of implementing popular will. Democracy is preferable to totalitarian systems because it is compatible with greater levels of choice and individual autonomy. But it is also a culturally and psychologically flawed system. Most obviously, the theory of democracy is not realized in practice. Indeed, democracy is only established and flourishes by reason of a sort of confidence trick.

Ernest Gellner uses two arguments to support this case.[1] First, democracy ignores the fact that society is based on social roles that result in an unequal division of authority and power. A brain surgeon may have the same voting rights as a window-cleaner, but invariably, the cultural capital, wealth and political influence of the former is superior to the latter. Second, democracy operates through institutions that employ professional, administrative and service workers. This salariat possesses interests of its own, which from time to time conflict with popular will and obstruct the implementation of democratic decisions.

The universal choice and equality implied by democratic theory is not accomplished in practice. In as much as this is so, it implies that the social and psychological condition of democracy consists of a generalized lack of fulfilment and satisfaction, since the cultural and economic promise implied by the political system is not experienced in the lived relations of culture and economy. Despite the legal recognition of equality between individuals, large sections of the democratized community, notably ethnic minorities, women and the disabled, do not have equal rights in practice. The suspicion that the system is not working and is not fair is a common characteristic in the body politic.

On the other hand, democracy permits levels of upward mobility unparalleled in other political and economic systems. It also creates high expectations of transparency in political transactions. It is more open to public scrutiny than other systems, and its elected representatives are more accountable for their actions than their counterparts in monarchical or totalitarian systems. This again reinforces the central symbolic importance of the elected leader in democracy. As the public face of the bureaucratic salariat, accountable finally to the electorate, the leader is the personification of the system.

The 'a priori' of Celebrity Culture

Robert Michels, perhaps best known for his thesis that 'the iron law of oligarchy' always rules democracy, is quite scathing about the electorate under democracy, arguing that the electorate is incapable of running its own affairs and must have a leader.[2] He identifies a 'cult of veneration' among the masses, and compares the electorate to 'idolators' who 'prostrate themselves' before leaders. Michels wrote from a state of frustration with the leadership of the German Democratic Party (SPD) which, he believed, had detached itself from party members and created a stifling culture of self-approval. His criticism was not confined to the SPD. Indeed, it was presented as an enquiry into the unintended consequences of democracy *per se*.

Michels made shrewd observations about the public face of democratic leaders. He allowed that the scale of modern urban–industrial society makes direct democracy impossible. The democratic ideal is therefore preserved by a representative system of decision-making in which leaders are elected to make decisions on behalf of the people. Those who are elected to the highest democratic offices are, in general, better educated and more eloquent than the rest of us. However, education and eloquence are not sufficient reasons for the acquisition of power. Another crucial asset is prestige. Indeed, Michels postulated (significantly, given the subject of this study), that 'the quality which most of all impresses the crowd is the prestige of celebrity'. For Michels, celebrity is not a consequence of political power, but a precondition of it. This proposition contributes to his criticism of democracy, since it suggests that democratic power is subject to celebrity culture, rather than prior and external to it.

If one thinks of the most revered political leaders of twentieth-century democracy this proposition is substantially verified. Theodore Roosevelt, De Gaulle, Churchill and Eisenhower were in the ancient tradition of soldier-politicians, who first acquired prestige on the battlefield. Kennedy's Presidential campaign publicized his heroic role in the PT-109 naval episode during the Second World War. George Bush, Edward Heath and James Callaghan were less meretricious in using their wartime experience for political gain, but each presented himself as a candidate with military experience that would enhance political leadership. With the decline of the warrior class, and the increasing fixation on technological systems in the conduct of warfare, the route to power of the soldier-politician is likely to be less prominent.

Thatcher, Blair and Clinton were all selected from backgrounds in the legal profession. The probability is that virtue in political celebrity already decisively derives from powers of legal-rational oratory and administration, rather than military excellence. This is just as Weber predicted in his analysis of the rationalization process. However, Reagan and Vaclav Havel became leaders in the USA and Czech Republic on the basis of the prestige acquired through the film and theatre. Perhaps this suggests that, in the twenty-first century, the arts will rival the professions and labour organizations as recruiting grounds for democratic leaders. The attempt in the late 1960s to lure Mick Jagger to stand as a Labour candidate for Parliament is a matter of record. Clint Eastwood has served as mayor in Carmel, California, and Warren Beatty has, on several occasions, most recently in 1999, expressed an interest in running for the Presidency. It is rash to predict a convergence between the political and entertainment wings of celebrity culture. On the other hand, the growing criticism in the West about the use of spin-doctors and 'Hollywood-style' party conferences suggests that politicians have borrowed much from film stars in matters of self-projection and manipulation of mass emotion.

If celebrity is becoming a precondition of attaining political power, it perhaps demonstrates the ubiquity of the celebrity race in contemporary society. Joshua Gamson refers to 'the celebrification process' in politics. By this term he means the acquisition by political leaders of the traits, conversational codes and presentational skills developed by Hollywood. Actually, as I noted in chapter Three, the celebrification process in American politics goes back further than Hollywood. Andrew Jackson, Abraham Lincoln and Ulysses S. Grant were all highly adept in self-projection and massaging public opinion. In 1877, when Grant visited Newcastle upon Tyne, it was reported that over 80,000 people crowded special trains and jammed the streets.[3] They received him as a global celebrity, a liberator of slaves and a friend of the working man. Grant was welcomed not simply as a former President, but as a titan of democracy who, at the time, radiated powerful connotations of glamour, freedom and the fulfilment of justice. The historical judgement on Grant has been modified somewhat since then. Many historians now regard him as an over-zealous military commander when crushing the Confederacy, and weak and vacillating during his Presidency. None the less, he was recognized as a man of the people, one who had emerged from the ranks of the producing class and, as such, provided a measure of achieved celebrity under democracy.

Gamson does not unpack in great detail what he means by the 'celebrification process', nor does he investigate it beyond the incursion of the conventions and practices of entertainment culture into the sphere of politics.[4] That the Hollywoodization of political culture has occurred is not in doubt. Political leaders are more sensitive to crowd-pleasing scripts and gestures, and party conventions conform to the conventions of spectacle required by the media. Al Gore's acceptance speech for the Presidential nomination at the Democratic Party convention in Los Angeles in August 2000 was a Hollywood set-piece of calculated self-deprecation and oily gratitude. Precariously, it followed Clinton's triumphant farewell address to the Convention, in which he nimbly skated over the terrain of moral turpitude and the deception of the public to emphasize the American economic miracle of 1992–2000. Gore's claim to be 'my own man' was designed to claim the moral high ground from Clinton's sexual peccadilloes while simultaneously gaining credit for the long economic boom achieved under the two Clinton administrations. Similarly, George W. Bush's inaugural speech in January 2001 deployed forms of projection and staged sincerity familiar to us from TV and film. In the UK, the annual Labour and Conservative party conferences have adopted the form of spectacle in which delegates play to the camera and spin-doctors fine-tune the proceedings to create positive mediagenic images.

The Celebrification Process

In confining celebrification to the Hollywoodization of political culture, Gamson somewhat undersells the concept. I take 'the celebrification process' to describe the general tendency to frame social encounters in mediagenic filters that both reflect and reinforce the compulsion of abstract desire. By the term *mediagenic* I mean elements and styles that are compatible with the conventions of self-projection and interaction, fashioned and refined by the mass-media. I argue that, from the development of national print culture in the eighteenth century, self-consciousness and the projection of identity have been themed by media representation and the compulsion of abstract desire. In summary, capitalism requires consumers to develop abstract desire for commodities. Desire is necessarily an abstract compulsion under capitalism, because the logic of economic accumulation means that it must be transferred in response to commodity and brand innovation. This abstract quality renders desire alienable from consumers, since they are routinely required to replace strong commodity wants with new ones. The compulsion of abstract desire under capitalism transforms the individual from a desiring object into a calculating object of desire. Consumers do not simply nourish wants for the commodity, they routinely construct the facade of embodiment in order to be desired by the abstracted mass. Fashion and taste cultures intensify and mirror this tendency.

Celebrity culture is therefore partly the expression of a cultural axis organized around abstract desire. It is an essential tool of commodification since it embodies desire. In particular, it provides consumers with compelling standards of emulation. On the other hand, the distance between celebrity and fan, and the constant innovation in celebrity culture, redouble the abstract quality in mass desire. Consumers under capitalism do not experience unifying fulfilment when desire is matched with possession. For the abstract quality of desire means that wants are never satisfied by possessing a particular commodity. Consumers are indeed split subjects. They are probably split along several axes, the most important of which, in celebrity culture, is the split between having and wanting. Contemporary culture's preoccupation with celebrity can partly be understood as an attempt to accomplish subjective integration, not by unifying the alienated parts of personality, but by subsuming alienated personality to the 'greater whole' of the public face of the celebrity.

This argument is composed of economic, political and cultural levels that need to be considered in greater detail. First, at the economic level, capitalism is the expropriation of surplus value as a standard feature of the labour process. However, to concentrate only on the labour theory of value distorts our understanding of capitalist economics. Expropriation is not the self-sufficient end of accumulation. One might say that expropriation only results in latent surplus value. In order for this value to be realized, capitalism must mobilize desire in the market-place.

What does it mean to mobilize desire? Classical psychoanalytic theory locates the seat of desire in the unconscious. Leaving aside the question of genetic influence, psychoanalytic theory maintains that the archetypal social relationship of desire is the dialogic bond between child and parent. Further, the child's transition to viable adulthood depends on the success-ful transference of desire onto a significant other, typically in the form of romantic love. Satisfactory transference therefore involves the replacement of one central dialogic relationship with another. That is, the bond between child and parent is replaced with the dialogic bond between two partners who voluntarily weave a bond of romantic love that is ideologically vali-dated as inalienable.

Now the global mobilization of desire requires attachments to be innovative, flexible and alienable. For accumulation is based in the compet-itive struggle between producers to maximize market share. Consumers are required to transfer allegiance in response to commodity and brand innovation. Just as global mobilization requires economic attachments to be innovative, flexible and alienable, it presupposes a mass communica-tion system that is reliable, versatile and ubiquitous. The foundations of this system were laid down in the eighteenth century. Given the economic logic of capitalist accumulation, it is no accident that the growth of this system inevitably resulted in the proliferation of fashion and taste cultures and the elevation of body culture and the public face in public life. With the development of an integrated transport system and a unified market, the basis for a unified audience, first nationally and later globally, was established.

The orthodox argument for the necessity of capitalism holds that the market is the most effective means of fulfilling consumer desire. In fact the opposite is the case. Capitalism can never permit desire to be fulfilled, since to do so will neutralize desire and thus, forfeit economic growth. Market organization is actually founded on the perpetual replenishment and development of desire through commodity and brand innovation. It requires consumers to cultivate abstract desire for commodities since the abstract form is most suitable for market mobilization. Capitalism demands that consumers consume, but it also requires them to be conscious of the built-in obsolescence of the commodity. All forms of consumption, then, have a provisional quality, which again reinforces the split between having and wanting in the consumer.

Celebrity culture is one of the most important mechanisms for mobilizing abstract desire. It embodies desire in an animate object, which allows for deeper levels of attachment and identification than with inanimate commodities. Celebrities can be reinvented to renew desire, and because of this they are extremely efficient resources in the mobilization of global desire. In a word, they *humanize* desire. In many cases the aging process works in their favour. For the fan-base ages with them, so that celebrities function not only as objects of abstract desire but as objects of nostalgia that can be further commodified by the market. The examples of Monroe, Dean, Presley, Lennon, Sinatra and Princess Diana demonstrate that death is not an impediment to additional commodification. Once the public face of the celebrity has been elevated and internalized in popular culture, it indeed possesses an immortal quality that permits it to be recycled, even after the physical death of the celebrity has occurred.

At the political level, one of the most significant developments in the growth of capitalist society was the reduction in the balance of power between the monarch and society in favour of the latter. The dynamics and variety of social form rather than the hallowed seigneurial grandeur of the established hierarchy gradually became the focus of politics and culture. Theoretically, democratic form increases everyone's opportunity for upward mobility. Of equal significance is the representation of opportunity and the character of achieved celebrity. Under democracy, the mobilization of desire is a mediated process in which professional marketing and public relations staff adorn the commodity with the symbolic garb designed to compel consumption. Mediation does not result in a dominant ideology of consumption in which social regulation is absolute. To assert the contrary is unsatisfactory, since it logically implies that the mass is non-reflexive and supine. Yet, unquestionably, mediation does thematize desire by concentrating collective consciousness on objects of desire embodied in celebrity culture. In the long run, the competitive principle results in more and more powers of mediation being confined to fewer and fewer people. In particular, corporations emerge as pivotal cultural impresarios in the mobilization of desire. This agglomeration of power is compatible with democracy since the principle of popular accountability is retained. None the less, practically speaking, the conduct of mass communications in mass democracy inevitably concentrates powers of cultural theming in the hands of specialists. Corporations and media personnel act not only as the gate-keepers of cultural data, but also as the originators of cultural debate, through the creation of celetoids and the packaging and repackaging of the public face of celebrities.

At the same time, the central political paradox of democracy is that the system formally delivering the means of equality and freedom to all cannot survive without generating structured inequalities of status and wealth. Celebrity culture is one of the most transparent expressions of this paradox. Achieved celebrities frequently hail from poor backgrounds, but their achievements drive a wedge between themselves and their audience. Thus, even in toasting the achievements of celebrities, fans are sharply conscious of the gulf between the staged life before them and their own bounded circumstances. Thus, under democracy, achieved celebrity is double-edged. It involves both the recognition of unusual characteristics in the celebrity, and the fateful realization that this recognition will elevate the celebrity further from the fan base. Achieved celebrity, one might say, begins as a recognition by fans of a wholeness and glamour that is missing from their own lives, and it reaches maturity in the apprehension that the elevation of the celebrity means leaving the fan behind. The split between having and wanting in the consumer is again reinforced. In as much as fans covet consummation with celebrities, the division between having and wanting may be experienced as an intolerable lack and produce psychopathological behaviour, such as stalking. While these cases are rare, they are statistically significant, and, as with serial killing and 'righteous slaughter', their incidence appears to be increasing decade on decade. This suggests negative cultural consequences between celebrity culture and the mobilization of abstract desire, and I will examine them presently. At this point it is necessary to dwell further on the political level of the general argument regarding celebrification. Democracy is a supple and adaptable political system. Celebrification has not simply resulted in the extension of the styles of embodiment and self-presentation developed in celebrity culture throughout the wider culture. It has also produced recognition and celebration of lifestyles, beliefs and forms of life previously unrecognized or repressed.

Life Politics and Celebrification

In seeking to make sense of the pattern of Western politics that followed the collapse of the Communist bloc in the late 1980s – the 'presently exist-ing socialist alternative', as Rudolf Bahro famously called it – Anthony Giddens fastens on the growing importance of what he calls 'life politics'.[5]

Life politics is a complex concept. At its heart is the proposition that the old emancipatory politics that focused on general, collective change and the ethics of universal equality, justice and participation has given way to a new politics predicated in the quest for self-actualization in the context of global interdependence. A decade earlier, Christopher Lasch noted the same quest, and explained it in terms of the cult of narcissism.[6] However, for Giddens, life politics is not a narcissistic programme of self-actualization. This is because it is clustered around a post-emancipatory ethic built on universal existential questions of respect for nature, tolerance of difference and the sanctity of freedom of choice.

Interestingly, Giddens proposes that the axial principle of life politics is embodiment. He argues that modernity has altered the boundaries of the body so that what he terms 'reflexive restructuring' is now a routine feature of ordinary social interaction. Reflexive restructuring means the continuous monitoring of public facades of identity and the utilization of elements from the public sphere to re-engineer the self in social encounters. Social cachet derives from holding the right opinions and cultivating the right body culture. In the age of life politics, individuals possess an accentuated awareness of the construction of the public face and appropriate material from public life to ensure that the right kind of match between self and society is achieved.

This is what celebrities do all the time, and it contributes to the common friction between the public face and veridical self in celebrity culture. While Giddens does not make the point explicitly, if it is now axiomatic that the body is no longer a given entity, the reflexive appropriation of bodily developments and processes draws heavily on celebrity culture. This is because celebrities are, to use Simmel's term again, the pre-eminent 'radioactive' resources for emulation in the body politic. 'Kylie' and 'Jason' suddenly became popular names in Britain during the 1980s, as parents named their children after Kylie Minogue and Jason Donovan from the popular Australian TV soap *Neighbours*. When

Princess Diana changed her hairstyle in an effort to look more mature and independent, it was widely copied. These may seem trivial examples. But naming and looking are important elements in social life. The reflexive restructuring at the heart of life politics constructs a facade that is designed to be celebrated by others. Celebrity culture is a primary resource in supplying strategies of reflexive restructuring with mediagenic components.

But this is not all there is to the relationship between life politics and celebrification. Life politics describes the resurgence of democracy because it champions the idea of the active agent and insists on the personal importance of everyone. It is a reaction against twentieth-century democracy, which tended to erase the special and unique qualities of the individual through bureaucracy and mass party organization. It is not akin to the radical revival of classical possessive individualism, since it proposes that self-actualization is enmeshed with universal moral and existential questions. These questions are concentrated in the domains of survival and being, individual and communal life, self-identity and science. Moreover, life politics takes it for granted that solutions to these questions can only be achieved through cooperation. In this sense, self-actualization is predicated in the recognition of social and cultural interdependence.

In addition, by insisting that everyone has special qualities that merit recognition and celebration in the body politic, life politics exposes the exclusionary logic of modern centralist politics. Indeed, an important claim Giddens makes is that the globalization of culture and economy require the reconstruction of the traditional notion of the nation state. In particular, multiculturalisms, the global flow of knowledge, culture and international finances destabilizes the image of the nation state as a unified racial entity sealed by hermetic walls of culture, security and national interest from the rest of the world. Globalization demands that we recognize local, national and international levels, but also acknowledge that these levels are porous.

One consequence of this is to reassess the forms of hierarchy and nomenclature associated with the governance systems established by the European nation states. The orientalist and postcolonial debates have elucidated the historical violence of the European and neo-European nation state, particularly in respect of race and sexuality. A notable feature of Western politics in the last 50 years has been the public recognition of lifestyles, beliefs and forms of practice that, earlier in the twentieth century, were marginalized or suppressed. Multiculturalism now celebrates ethnicities. Feminism celebrates the strength of women. The disabled are now recognized as full members of the body politic rather than as shadowy presences, off-loaded to the periphery of public culture. And gays and lesbians have achieved legal recognition. Of course, prejudicial beliefs and practices against ethnicities, women, the disabled and gays and lesbians are still encountered, but their prejudicial nature can now be legally challenged and condemned. This is a volte-face from the situation in the 1950s, when exclusionary systems and practices against ethnicities, women, the disabled and gays and lesbians abounded, often with the covert support of the law. Of course I accept that legal recognition of status is not equivalent to social recognition. The continuing vitality of social movements against racial, sexual and bodily prejudice confirms what ordinary reflexive monitoring frequently observes, which is that prejudice persists. However, there has been an earthquake in the social terrain of belonging and recognition over the last half-century. The exclusionary logic of nation state systems of governance has been breached, and exclusion from full participation in the body politic on grounds of race, sexuality or health is no longer socially acceptable.

Turning now to examine the cultural level more directly, two broad issues need to be separated. First, in respect of life politics and celebrification, it is now argued that the recognition of marginality has resulted in the undifferentiated celebration of difference, thus reversing the earlier democratic gains achieved through challenging exclusion. Amitai Etzioni and Todd Gitlin, the one a somewhat naïve exponent of communitarianism, the other a distinguished Left-wing critic, are odd bedfellows, but both have argued, albeit from contrasting theoretical traditions, that political correctness is in some respects counter-productive. Of the two critiques, Gitlin's is more sophisticated.[7] Etzioni calls for the revival of community around binding values that he holds to be transparent and universal.[8] His version of communitarianism is ultimately nostalgic because it fails to address the situated position of the actor, omits to demonstrate either transparency or universality, and cannot explain social change.

In contrast, Gitlin's approach recognizes the situated position of the actor and analyses change as the expression of power struggles. He holds that the recognition of diversity began from good and valid arguments focusing on the exclusionary aspects of citizenship under the nation state. However, the affirmation of the rights of minorities has exaggerated differences and attenuated common interests. In celebrating repressed voices and excluded histories, diversity has affirmed the virtues of the margins while failing to address the centres of power. For Gitlin, the Left's traditional object of building a larger future for all has been exchanged for a patchwork of 'competing respect cultures', in which honorific status is claimed by each and every one of these cultures on the basis of their historical marginalization. It does not follow from this that respect for minority cultures is misplaced. On the contrary, Gitlin holds that the recognition of difference is a laudable part of the democratic process. However, when difference between respect cultures is automatically celebrated, and when excluded history is instantly culturally prioritized, the power of the commons dwindles. Corporate capitalism has reinvented itself in the age of infotech, while counter-cultures have become hamstrung by debates around respect hierarchies and the parameters of cultural dignity.

Gitlin's argument is important because it seizes on the divisive aspects of celebrification in life politics. Exponents of life politics frequently skate over these aspects on the pretext that, in view of the exclusionary injustices of history, the celebrification of minorities is worthy and good *per se*. Gitlin succeeds in revealing the shallowness of this well-intentioned standpoint. Further, he provides a timely reminder of the strategic significance of the commons in challenging oppression.

The second issue that needs to be distinguished refers to the cultural consequences of abstract desire. What does abstract desire mean in relation to celebrity culture? In the first place it means possessing deep attraction for given celebrities that as a result remould both lifestyle and embodiment. I use the term abstract to highlight the subconscious nature of this desire. The passion that fans feel for celebrities is not merely a matter of cherishing the technical accomplishments or the aesthetic public face of the celebrity. Rather it springs from subconscious levels, in both the fan and fan culture. It suggests an absence or lack in existence which is probably ultimately related to the decline of organized religion. In mobilizing desire for the celebrity, fans are also articulating a lack in themselves and in the culture around them.

But to focus only on the depth of fan attachments to celebrities produces a one-sided understanding of the dynamics of abstract desire. What also must be stressed is the diffuse character of abstract desire. It is diffuse in at least two senses. First, it is not confined to the technical accomplishments or aesthetic public face of the celebrity, but extends to emotional, sexual, spiritual and existential identification with the celebrity. In extreme cases the veridical self of the fan voluntarily submits to be substantially engulfed by the public face of the celebrity. This can lead to hopeless and painful feelings of resignation when the imaginary relationship with the celebrity is unconsummated, or to aggressive feelings of resentment against the celebrity. However, a distinctive feature of abstract desire is its capacity to diffuse into every aspect of the fan's life, taking over the responsibilities of work, family and even bodily health. This suggests that the defences against incursion by a desired external object are not strong. In building up strong receptivity to celebrity and commodity culture, capitalism and democracy produce weakly integrated personalities who are vulnerable to external attraction and its vagaries. Over the long run, fan attachment to a given celebrity is rarely exclusive and lifelong. The competitive principle in the market renews celebrity culture and elicits the transference of desire to new celebrity figures. Promiscuity, one might say, is built into abstract desire. The logic of capitalist accumulation requires it to be transferable, and the split between having and wanting in the consumer means that the fan is, perhaps usually subconsciously, always craving transference.

The second sense in which abstract desire is diffuse refers to the facade of embodiment we construct as an ordinary part of identity work. Abstract desire requires the individual to be desirable in order to stand the highest chances of attracting a mate. Although the ideal of romantic love enjoins the individual to limit desire to one mate, the facade of embodiment we construct is designed to be multi-attractive. We need to be desirable to the abstracted mass, because it is in the nature of desire to be transferable and hence alienable. One implication of this is that even voluntarily chosen romantic attachments are treated as ultimately provisional, so that the cultivation of a multi-attractive facade decreases our chance of being alone if a romantic attachment fails. The increase in the rate of divorce, the growth of long-term cohabitation and the rise in pre-nuptial marriage agreements on economic entitlement all support this argument. The facade of embodiment is divided between a favoured self-image and a public face acknowledged to be artificial and 'designing', in the sense of seeking to create an impression. Celebrification therefore divides us psychologically along two fronts. First, we are divided between the favoured self-image and the veridical self. Second, we are estranged from the artificial public face constructed in social encounters because we are aware that the construction is provisional, and hence liable to disruption.

The psychological pressure that derives from these divisions is expressed in the most intense form in celebrity culture. This is because celebrities derive their entire power from maintaining a public face that fans will recognize and honour.

Celebrification is the corollary of a reward culture in which individuals are differentiated from one another by monetary and status distinction. Democracy requires not only formal electoral equality, but the layering of ranks of honorific culture.

Democratic ideology, which claims to create more opportunities for upward mobility and subjective success than other political systems, constructs the reproachful and instructive example of the successful. It is instructive because, as Samuel Smiles grasped, achieved celebrity presents standards of emulation for the mass. It is reproachful because everyone knows that there is no necessary connection between merit and achievement. Celebrity culture includes celetoids as well as great writers, scientists, artists, actors, musicians, models, sportsmen and women, orators and politicians. Celebrity culture is the result of the momentous change in the public sphere when the hectic, prolific, transmuting character of social form became recognized as the core of cultural consciousness. Media wars produce not only the representation of social form but the magnification and dramatization of pseudo-events. Hence, in part, the prominence of celetoids in contemporary culture.

It is an enormous paradox that democracy, the system which claimed moral superiority on the basis of extending equality and freedom to all, cannot proceed without creating celebrities who stand above the common citizen and achieve veneration and god-like worship. It is easy to deplore this state of affairs, as Pierre Bourdieu does in his sally against media celebrities.[9] But it is also rash to do so. Celebrity culture is the expression of social form. The grotesque, bloated cultural shape assumed by some of our celebrities is the development of the common constituents of social form. As long as democracy and capitalism prevail there will always be an

Olympus, inhabited not by Zeus and his court, but by celebrities, elevated from the mass, who embody the restless, fecund and frequently disturbing form of the mass in the public face they assemble.

References

One: Celebrity and Celetoids

1 G. H. Mead, *Mind, Self and Society* (Chicago, 1934).
2 P. Bourdieu, *On Television and Journalism* (London, 1996), p. 46.
3 D. Boorstin, *The Image* (London, 1961), pp. 38–9.
4 J. Baudrillard, *Simulations* (New York, 1983).
5 Dick Pountain and David Robins, *Cool Rules: Anatomy of an Attitude* (London, 2000), p. 19.
6 See I. Ang, *Watching Dallas* (London, 1985).
7 Max Weber, *The Theory of Social and Economic Organization* (New York, 1947).
8 H. Marcuse, *One Dimensional Man* (London, 1964).
9 H. Marcuse, *The Aesthetic Dimension* (London, 1978).
10 See G. Debord, *The Society of the Spectacle* (London, 1967).
11 E. Morin, *The Stars* (New York, 1960).
12 K. Anger, *Hollywood Babylon* (New York, 1975) and *Hollywood Babylon 2* (London, 1984).
13 M. Foucault, *The Order of Things* (London, 1970).
14 D. Marshall, *Celebrity and Power* (Minneapolis, 1997).
15 Gabriel Tarde, *La Logique sociale* (Paris, 1895); Gustave Le Bon, *The Crowd: A Study of the Popular Mind* (New York, 1901).

16 Marshall, *Celebrity and Power*, p. 243.

17 P. Biskind, *Easy Riders, Raging Bulls* (London, 1998).

18 J. Gamson, *Claims to Fame* (Berkeley, CA, 1994), p. 195.

19 In O. Klapp, *Heroes, Villains and Fools* (Englewood Cliffs, NJ, 1962).

20 E. Goffman, *Behaviour in Public Places* (London, 1963), and Goffman, *Interaction Ritual* (New York, 1967).

21 G. Studlar, *The Mad Masquerade* (New York, 1996).

22 R. Dyer, *Heavenly Bodies* (London, 1986), p. 17.

23 R. deCordova, *Picture Personalities* (Urbana, IL, 1990).

24 R. Dyer, *Heavenly Bodies* (London, 1986).

Two: Celebrity and Religion

1 See F. Vermorel & J. Vermorel, *Starlust* (London, 1985).

2 Keith Thomas, *Religion and the Decline of Magic* (London, 1971)

3 M. Eliade, *Shamanism* (London, 1964).

4 Eliade, *Shamanism* p. 511.

5 E. Durkheim, *The Elementary Forms of Religious Life* (New York, 1915).

6 In N. Gabler, *Life: The Movie* (New York, 1998).

7 D. Riesman, *The Lonely Crown* (New York, 1950).

8 Cited in J. Fowles, *Starstruck* (Washington, DC, 1992), p. 192.

9 E. Morin, *The Stars* (New York, 1960), pp. 38–9.

10 G. McCann, *Marilyn Monroe* (London, 1996), p. 199.

11 M. Faithfull, *Faithfull* (London, 1994), p. 191.

12 In C. Lasch, *The Culture of Narcissism* (London, 1980).

Three: Celebrity and Aestheticization

1 Roy Porter, *English Society in the Eighteenth Century* (Harmondsworth, 1982), pp. 250–52, for my details on newspaper, magazine and book publishing.

2 Mary Douglas, *Purity and Danger* (London, 1966).

3 K. Woolf, ed., *The Sociology of Georg Simmel* (New York, 1950).
4 See J. Keane, *Tom Paine* (London, 1995).
5 John Brewer, *The Pleasures of the Imagination* (London, 1997).
6 S. Smiles, *Self Help* (London, 1859), p. 21.
7 Nathaniel Hawthorne, in J. Mellon, *The Face of Lincoln* (New York, 1979).
8 Cited in C. Fleming, *High Concept* (London, 1998), p. 64.

Four: Celebrity and Transgression

1 R. Merton, *Social Theory and Social Structure* (New York, 1968).
2 J. Katz, *Seductions of Crime* (New York, 1988).
3 E. Leyton, *Hunting Humans* (Toronto, 1995).
4 N. Gabler, *Life: The Movie* (New York, 1988).
5 Orwell's essay, first published in *The Tribune* in February 1946, can be found in the Penguin edition of *The Decline of the English Murder and Other Essays* (London, 1965).
6 D. Thomson, *A Biographical Dictionary of Film* (London, 1994), p. 678.
7 Katz, *Seductions of Crime*, p. 12.
8 Quoted in S. Cohen and L. Taylor, *Escape Attempts* (London, 1976), p. 177.
9 E. Goffmann, Interaction Ritual (New York, 1967).
10 Miles Davis, *Miles* (London, 1989), p. 48.
11 Quoted in B. Paris, *Louise Brooks* (London, 1991), pp. 393, 395–6.
12 Quoted in G. McCann, *Cary Grant* (London, 1996), p. 176.
13 In McCann, *Cary Grant*, p. 177.

Five: Celebrity and Celebrification

1 Ernest Gellner, *Conditions of Liberty: Civil Society and its Rivals* (London, 1994).
2 Robert Michels, *Political Parties* (New York, 1915).
3 W. S. McFeely, *Grant: A Biography* (New York, 1982), p. 184.
4 J. Gamson, *Claims to Fame* (Berkeley, CA, 1994)

5 A. Giddens, *Modernity and Self Identity* (Cambridge, 1991).

6 C. Lasch, *The Culture of Narcissism* (London, 1980).

7 Todd Gitlin, *The Twilight of Common Dreams* (New York, 1995).

8 Amitai Etzioni, *The Spirit of Community* (New York, 1994).

9 P. Bourdieu, *On Television and Journalism* (London, 1996).

Bibliography

T. Adorno and M. Horkheimer, *Dialectic of Enlightenment* (London, 1944)

K. Anger, *Hollywood Babylon* (New York, 1975)

—, *Hollywood Babylon 2* (London, 1984)

P. Biskind, *Easy Riders, Raging Bulls* (London, 1998)

L. Braudy, *The Frenzy of Renown* (New York, 1997)

J. Brewer, *The Pleasures of the Imagination* (London 1997)

S. Bruce, *Pray TV* (London, 1990)

T. Cowen, *What Price Fame?* (New York, 2000)

G. Debord, *The Society of the Spectacle* (London, 1967)

R. deCordova, *Picture Personalities* (Urbana, IL, 1990)

R. Dyer, *Heavenly Bodies* (London, 1986)

—, *Stars* (London, 1998)

M. Eliade, *Patterns of Comparative Religion* (New York, 1958)

A. Elliott, *The Mourning of John Lennon* (Berkeley, CA, 1999)

N. Gabler, *Life: The Movie* (New York, 1998)

A. Giddens, *Modernity and Self Identity* (Cambridge, 1991)

D. Giles, *Illusions of Immortality* (London, 2000)

E. Goffman, *Behaviour in Public Places* (London, 1963)

—, *Interaction Ritual* (New York, 1967)

M. Gottdiener, *The Theming of America* (Boulder, CO, 1997)

O. Klapp, *Heroes, Villains and Fools* (Englewood Cliffs, NJ, 1962)

S. Kracauer, *Theory of Film* (New York, 1960)

—, *The Mass Ornament* (New York, 1995)

C. Lasch, *The Culture of Narcissism* (London, 1980)

K. Lewis, *The Assassination of Lincoln* (New York, 1994)

R. Lewis, *The Life and Death of Peter Sellers* (London, 1994)

E. Leyton, *Hunting Humans* (Toronto, 1995)

D. Lyon, *Jesus in Disneyland* (Cambridge, 2000)

G. Marcus, *Dead Elvis* (London, 1991)

H. Marcuse, *One Dimensional Man* (London, 1964)

R. Merton, *Social Theory and Social Structure* (New York, 1968)

D. Riesman, *The Lonely Crowd* (New York, 1950)

G. Rodman, *Elvis after Elvis* (London, 1996)

C. Rojek, *Leisure and Culture* (London, 2000)

R. Schickel, *Intimate Strangers* (New York, 1985)

G. Studlar, *The Mad Masquerade* (New York, 1996)

J. Tagg, *The Burden of Representation* (London, 1988)

F. Vermorel and J. Vermorel, *Starlust* (London, 1985)

M. Weber, *The Theory of Social and Economic Organization* (New York, 1947)

G. Wills, *John Wayne's America* (New York, 1997)

L. Yablonsky, *Gangsters* (New York, 1997)

Acknowledgements

In July 1999 Peter Hamilton persuaded me over lunch in *The Ivy* restaurant, London, to write this book. Later, he also read the manuscript, and proved that the publishing world lost a trenchant, but fair, editor when he opted for an academic career.

Celebrity was written in tandem with *Society and Culture: Principles of Scarcity and Solidarity*, a book co-authored with Bryan Turner. Bryan's intellectual comradeship and standards of craftsmanship have become more central to me over the years, and I thank him for his friendship and example. Academics have, of course, developed their own celebrity culture and, in the role of fan, I have been fortunate to enjoy friendship with, and intellectual sustenance from, Peter Beilharz, Roger and Carl Bromley, Alan Bryman, Ellis Cashmore, Eric Dunning, Mike Featherstone, David Frisby, Doug Kellner, Lauren and Judy Langman, Jim McGuigan, John O'Neill, Maggie O'Neill, George Ritzer, Chris Shilling, Barry Smart, Keith Tester and John Tomlinson.

At Nottingham Trent I have had the wise support and comradeship of Stephen Chan, Deborah Chambers, Sandra Harris, Richard Johnson, Ali Mohamaddi and Patrick Williams. My PhD students, Kerry Featherstone and Vanessa Gill-Brown, are set to become, I have no doubt, academic celebrities of distinction, and I thank them and my undergraduate students on the 'Leisure and Popular Culture' course for their intellectual verve and fellowship.

Finally, thanks again to Gerry, Sam, Luke and Robert, the four principal celebrities in my life.

List of Illustrations

Cover: Rafik Kashopov as Elvis at the Lenin Monument, St Petersburg, July 1992. Photo: © Gary Matoso (Contact Press Images).

p. 8: Rudolph Valentino and Vilma Banky in a postcard from the 'Famous Cinema Star' series. Photo: Mary Evans Picture Library.

p. 50: The window of the 24 Hour Church of Elvis in Portland, Oregon.

p. 100: Divine Brown and Hugh Grant, as posed by the Los Angeles Police Department in June 1995.

p. 142: Hippy cult leader and murderer Charles Manson in confinement.

p. 180: Icelandic musician and film actor Björk.